# *Working Class Housing on Tyneside 1850 – 1939*

*Bill Lancaster,*
*Editor*

*Bewick Press*

First published 1994
by the Bewick Press
132 Claremont Road
Whitley Bay
Tyne and Wear
NE26 3TX



ISBN 0-9516056-7-4

Printed and Bound in Great Britain by
Roger Booth Associates, Half Moon Chambers,
10 Bigg Market, Newcastle upon Tyne NE1 1UW.

# Contents

## Acknowledgements

The editor and contributors wish to thank staff of Gateshead, Newcastle upon Tyne, North Tyneside and South Tyneside libraries for their assistance and unstinting service during the preparation of this book. Several of the authors are also indebted to the staff of Tyne and Wear Archive Service for guidance through the Archive's considerable holdings. We all gratefully acknowledge the permission received from the above institutions to reproduce illustrative material from their collections. Angela McGregor and Kathleen Mensforth patiently tolerated the idiosyncrasies of the authors in their preparation of the manuscript. The Bewick Press encouraged this project from its inception and have proved unflagging in their support. Needless to say any faults are the responsibility of the authors.

# INTRODUCTION

The history of working class housing on Tyneside over the last one hundred and fifty years reflects both national trends and patterns of unique development. England's most overcrowded conurbation in the nineteenth century has often produced some of the most ambitious responses to the housing problem. But housing for the working class has always been more than a relationship between need and provision. Housing is, and has been throughout the period, a highly charged political topic. National governments since the public health reforms of the mid-nineteenth century have with varying degrees of enthusiasm attempted to shape the form, quality and quantity of the popular housing stock. Yet the fiat of Westminster up until the second world war was always the subject of local negotiation and implementation. Even the more generous provisions contained in the Acts of 1919, 1930 and 1935, and John Wheatley's famous subsidy from the first Labour government were met with a variegated local response. The experience of Tyneside in the provision of public sector housing in the inter-war period graphically illustrates this point. To overgeneralise somewhat the south bank communities of Tyneside were far more enthusiastic providers of public housing between the wars than their counterparts across the river.

This contrast is all the more sharp when we bear in mind that the communities on both banks of the river were paying some of the highest rent levels in England for the country's smallest dwelling units. The differing fortunes of the inter-war Labour Party is the major factor in accounting for this contrast but we must also not lose sight of those deeply embedded interests that were hostile to the public provision of housing. Indeed from the perspective of the present it is salutary to remember than public housing for general needs was government policy for less than two decades of the last century and a half. There has been no 'Long March of Labour' in the quest to house workers on Tyneside. There has, however, been some notable local triumphs. Beacon Lough sits elegantly on Gateshead Fell, a living testimony to the ideals of an early generation of housing planners and the generosity of the Wheatly subsidies. Blaydon Council in the inter-war period pursued a policy of greatly improving the town's appalling housing stock with an ambitious house building scheme and by employing direct labour helped relieve local unemployment. More recently the Byker Wall has been subject to international acclaim. Unfortunately the downside is just as impressive. The Meadowell is now a national symbol of public housing decline and social strife. Similar areas can be found in the West End of Newcastle, Noble Street in Elswick and the tower blocks at Felling have been demolished while St Cuthbert's village Gateshead, built as recently as the 1970's, awaits the bulldozer and Jimmy Forsyth's camera.

To a great extent Tyneside's housing development during the twentieth century has been a response to gross overcrowding caused by the ubiquity of the Victorian built Tyneside flat. As Kit Pearce demonstrates in his essay the genesis of this housing form in extremely complex and is not reducible to simple factor analysis. Economics, politics, culture and the experience of ordinary people interacted within the umbrella of local circumstance to produce this unique dominant type. Indeed we need to remember, as Pearce saliently points out, that the Tyneside flat was itself a response to an earlier crisis. Moreover, this housing form has proved enduringly popular. Perhaps no longer suitable, the smaller ones at least, for family accommodation, they remain highly useful for students, singles and couples and give the region an added flexibility in meeting housing needs.

The debate over the introduction of Tyneside flats was centred in Newcastle and it comes as no surprise that Newcastle's faith in the power of the private sector was tenacious. The efficiency of self-help, a powerful building and landlord lobby, a weak administrative structure and the long absence of working class voices rendered the city council reluctant travellers down the path of municipal housing. As Michael Barke and Maureen Callcott show in their essay Newcastle's response to an appalling housing situation during the Victorian and Edwardian period is not one that the city can be proud of.

The persistence of faith in self-help and the private sector proved fertile ground for those inter-war advocates of a property owning democracy that included at least a part of the working class. Tyneside with its experience of deep economic decline during this period at first glance appears to be an unlikely area for this strategy which is generally associated with southern England and the then prosperous midlands. There were, however, pockets of prosperity in the conurbation particularly amongst workers employed in the expanding electrical generation industry. Thus examples of working class home ownership in the 1930's pepper the local housing stock. Walkerville was popular with workers from Parson's and similar areas can be found in Hebburn, the location of many Reyrolles employees. David Byrne in his essay uses a rich variety of source material, including building society records, to analyse the complexity of the local process of early working class home-ownership and compares this with the national picture.

In terms of quality the inter-war period made notable contributions to Tyneside's housing stock with the 1930's semi and the Wheatly estates. There were, however, other developments which detract from the period's benign image, at least in terms of housing. The Meadowell estate in North Shields is a national symbol of inner-city decline, social deprivation and violence. Michael Barke and Guy Turnbull in their essay explore the origins of the Meadowell phenomena and locate the source of the problem not in the quality of the housing, nor the 'nature' of the residents but in the attitude of local society to slum clearance programmes. This interpretation challenges many of the myths that surround the Meadowell and highlights the endurance of the Victorian distinction between the deserving and 'undeserving' poor, a distinction that has been revived over the last decade with bitter consequences.

Finally the editor and authors of this volume are well aware that this book is not a comprehensive study of Tyneside housing during the period under review. Gaps are all too obvious. There is need for work on areas only alluded to in the following pages: miners' housing, other inter-war estates, the role and activities of the North East Housing Association in the 1930's and a more detailed analysis of the changing geography of the local housing stock. Unfortunately the decline in research funding for social history and social science and the even more worrying decline in the number of young scholars entering these fields offers little prospect for a comprehensive study appearing in the near future. Hopefully this short collection will stimulate interest in this important area of the region's history.

BILL LANCASTER

## Guide to Further Reading

All the essays are appended with specialised bibliographies. For those readers, perhaps unfamiliar with the region, who require a general overview of Tyneside the following should prove useful:


R Colls and B Lancaster, (eds)
Geordies Roots of Regionalism
Edinburgh, 1992.

C M Fraser and K Emsley
Tyneside
Newton Abbot, 1973.

M McCord
North East England, The Regions Development 1760 - 1960
London, 1979.

H A Mess
Industrial Tyneside,
London, 1928.

S Middlesbrook Newcastle upon Tyne
Its Growth and Achievement,
Newcastle upon Tyne, 1950.

D J Rowe 'The North East' in F M L Thompson (ed)
The New Cambridge Social History
volume I The Regions
Cambridge 1990.

**MUNICIPAL INTERVENTION IN HOUSING : CONSTRAINTS AND DEVELOPMENTS IN NEWCASTLE UPON TYNE, 1835-1914**

The fact that municipal authorities actually did possess quite wide powers of intervention in housing at the end of the nineteenth century is a point that bears some repetition in view of the generally low level of such intervention. The Artisans' and Labourers' Dwellings Act of 1868 enabled local authorities to demolish individual unfit dwellings. The Artisans' and Labourers' Dwellings and Improvement Act of 1875 enlarged the scope of such activity to include groups of dwellings and also gave municipalities powers to build replacement accommodation. The Public Health Act of 1875 extended to all local authorities the powers to establish bye-laws governing the standards of new building. Finally, the Housing of the Working Classes Act of 1890, whilst consolidating earlier legislation on slum clearance, in Part III gave local authorities the powers to build houses for general needs. Thus, from 1890 onwards, the municipal authorities had, ostensibly at least, the powers to control standards of new housing, to carry out slum clearance and build replacement houses, and to build houses to rent.

If the powers to act were available, the will to do so was, in many cases, notably absent (Smith et al, 1986). Some of the general reasons for this inertia have been well rehearsed. For example, the Artisans' and Labourers' Dwellings Improvement Act of 1875 gave no assistance to finance the building of replacement accommodation and local authorities had to dispose of any dwellings within ten years of their construction (Gauldie, 1974). Similarly, the 1890 Act provided no central government subsidies to build council houses and most local councillors were antipathetic towards increasing the rates to pay for council housing. The frequently stated view in the municipal council chambers was that it was not the local authority's job to become involved in housing. Yet such a view frequently and conveniently ignored the fact that many large city councils were historically substantial property owners and landlords.

If some of the general factors militating against municipal involvement in housing are well known, it is becoming increasingly clear from a range of studies that considerable local variation existed in responses to housing problems and to national housing legislation. Indeed, such variation was inevitable when most of the national legislation on housing and related matters was of an 'enabling' nature and therefore subject to wide variations of interpretation and intensity of application in the provincial council chambers. The introduction of bye-laws represented the most widespread, if limited, type of intervention and has been admirably covered by Daunton (1984) but Ashworth (1954) had earlier drawn attention to the fact that where such bye-laws existed the degree of rigour in their enforcement varied widely between municipalities. From the mid nineteenth century a number of municipal authorities legislated to obtain powers of compulsory acquisition, clearance and redevelopment of slum property. Accounts of such policies include studies of Glasgow (Allen, 1965) and Edinburgh (Smith, 1980). As noted above such powers were eventually extended to all English municipalities under the 1875 Artisans' and Labourers' Dwellings Improvement Act, producing schemes in Birmingham (Briggs, 1952) Liverpool (Taylor, 1974) and London (Yelling, 1981). The 1890 Housing of the Working Classes Act attempted to extend the possibilities for municipal intervention. Although the Act did not add greatly to the existing powers available to local authorities, the power to raise loans to finance slum clearance and rebuilding being already available, it did consolidate previous legislation in a comprehensive manner and served to stimulate activity in a number of towns and cities. Liverpool (Pooley, 1985) was amongst the most enthusiastic local authorities and schemes in Sheffield (Gaskell, 1976) and Manchester (Harrison, 1981) were also initiated. It has been suggested that in total over 170 local authorities used the powers of the 1890 Act to intervene in housing in the areas of their jurisdiction (Pooley, op cit).

This chapter seeks to explore the nature of the response of one local authority - Newcastle upon Tyne - to housing issues before the First World War. In the belief that the response to the formal housing legislation of the last quarter of the nineteenth century can only be appreciated by reference to earlier events, the study is extended back to the formation of the 'reformed' Corporation in 1835. It is intended to show the scale of inertia in the face of massive problems but, more particularly, to explore some of the reasons for non-intervention despite the existence of available powers and the clear manifestations of housing problems by any criteria adopted.

## Urban Growth in Nineteenth Century Newcastle upon Tyne

Numerous contemporaries, both citizens and visitors, condemned housing conditions at regular intervals in nineteenth century Newcastle. The city had a "housing problem" by which is meant extreme overcrowding, insanitary conditions, dangerously unhealthy public space, high rents and a shortage of affordable accommodation for a substantial part of the population. The problem had many dimensions and causes but the latter are founded in industrial and technological developments, population growth and the disparity between the wages of the large numbers of labourers and the rents which had to be paid. The population figures suggest a dramatic change in the environment. In the first half of the nineteenth century, the population in the area controlled by Newcastle Corporation more than trebled from 28,294 to 87,784 and more than doubled again to reach 226,000 by 1911. The expansion first of coal mining, then of heavy industry and ship building attracted migrant workers at an ever increasing rate. This population boom was not evenly spread and was most dramatic in the east and west of the city along the river banks at Elswick and Westgate and Byker during the second half of the century (Rowe, 1977).

**TABLE 1**

**POPULATION CHANGE IN NEWCASTLE UPON TYNE REGISTRATION DISTRICT *, 1851-1901**

| | Total Population | Change | % Change | Natural Change | Migration |
|---|---|---|---|---|---|
| 1851 | 87156 | - | - | - | - |
| 1861 | 110968 | +21812 | +24.5 | +8300 | +13512 |
| 11871 | 131198 | +20230 | +18.2 | +13975 | +6255 |
| 11881 | 150252 | +19054 | +14.5 | +19755 | -701 |
| 11891 | 196817 | +46565 | +31.0 | +24189 | +22376 |
| 11901 | 233644 | +36827 | +18.7 | +28363 | +8464 |

* Data for the Registration District - a slightly larger unit than the city.

Table 1 gives some indication of the demographic pressure upon housing in the second half of the nineteenth century. The data relate to the Registration District of Newcastle upon Tyne, a somewhat larger area than the city proper. Nevertheless, the two areas correspond sufficiently for us to make some meaningful observations. Population growth peaked in the 1880s but, significantly, this was after a substantial reduction in the rate of population growth in the 1870s. As Table 1 shows, this was largely a result of a negative migration balance. In the next decade, however, there was a major turn around with a massive migration gain of 22,000 people. Demographic pressure upon accommodation was therefore not consistent throughout this period. Even if we ignore the rate of new household formation within the city, the net migration statistics reveal something of the fluctuating pressure upon housing. Clearly, this must have been substantial in the 1850s, reduced somewhat in the 1860s and slackened in the 1870s. As migrants represent the most obvious and "visible" demand for additional accommodation it is tempting to speculate whether by the 1870s and early 1880s a certain complacency may have occurred. If so, the rest of the century shows how misguided such an attitude could be, with the 1880s recording a major influx of migrants and the 1890s the highest absolute natural increase in population. The population data, therefore, seem to indicate two periods of significant additional pressure on housing - the 1850s-60s and the 1880s-90s. In addition to this, of course, there remained the fundamental issue of the overall adequacy of existing housing stock in terms of numbers and quality.

While housing provision, as has been stated, was recognized by a variety of observers as seriously inadequate in nineteenth century Newcastle, the question of responsibility was rarely faced. In a different ideological climate, while fortunes were being amassed by entrepreneurs unrestricted by regulation, self-help was the order of the day. From time to time, as we shall see, housing conditions were brought to the attention of the town council (Newcastle became a city in 1882) but they were never a major preoccupation during the nineteenth century. There was no inexorable momentum of intervention leading to any sort of radically amended view of local government's role in the matter. Public provision of a large part of the housing stock was a twentieth century development and the norm of rented accommodation provided by private enterprise for profit was rarely questioned. Thus when we explore the responses to public challenges what we find is a series of marginal shifts evolved in circumstances of particular pressure. To illustrate this contention, some of the challenges and responses will be examined.

Revelations and Responses 1844-1874

In the first half of the nineteenth century, the larger part of additional accommodation needed was provided by the sub-division of existing property and the insertion of new housing within the already built up area (Barke and Buswell, 1980). Later the town spread beyond the medieval walls which had contained it for centuries. Property development was not interfered with by the corporation, many of whose members were considerable property owners, as was the corporation itself (Benwell Community Project, 1978), but the condition of the inhabitants of over-crowded homes became a wider health hazard and it was this which received considerable, though intermittent, publicity. There was never any shortage of accommodation for those who could afford to pay the prices which would provide acceptable returns to speculative builders (Whitburn, 1902). The middle classes left the centre of the town and the banks of the Tyne and estates were built within easy reach of the factories and the city centre for coal-owners, financiers and large scale industrialists in Old Benwell, Elswick and Jesmond. In the city old property was sub-divided and further sub-divided, accommodation was scarce and over-crowding perhaps the most notorious in England. Commissioner Reid, drawing up his Health of Towns Report for the first Royal Commission on the subject, requested the Council to provide information on various aspects of the subject and it was made public knowledge for the first time. This was in 1844 (Reid, 1845), and the Report of the Cholera Commission ten years later provided further revelations (Cholera Inquiry Commission, 1854). Also during the 1840s and 1850s local Sanitary Associations and clergy (Newcastle Corporation Proceedings, 1848) petitioned the Council to implement powers obtained in local Improvement Acts, while in 1849 sanitary reformers memorialised the General Board of Health to bring the 1848 Public Health Act into operation in Newcastle by virtue of the high mortality rate of 29.9% for the last seven years (PRO, MH13/323). This was followed by an inquiry conducted by the Board of Health's Inspector Rawlinson in 1849. He included "fearful over-crowding.....in the houses of the poor" as a major cause of the town's high death rate (Rawlinson, 1853). This report was, most unusually, not written up for three years and was never printed and published. It remains in manuscript. In 1850 the Newcastle Chronicle published a series of articles on the condition of the poor and in 1861 an article in The Builder declared, "Cologne has a bad name; Cairo has an even worse reputation; but that part of Newcastle called Sandgate must be allowed to exceed either city in stenches, filth, over-crowding and pestilential ills" (The Builder, 1861, p.242). The revelations which followed one another during the 1850s concentrated upon specific areas and emphasised the plight of a particular group - the very poorest in contemporary society - whose living conditions contrasted ever more sharply with those of the better paid. From at least about 1870 onwards, the skilled worker who enjoyed a rise in real wages could afford the higher rents of new bye-law housing, often in the shape of Tyneside flats. Additionally, a number of large employers began to follow the tradition of colliery owners and build houses for their work force.

In 1850 an article in the Newcastle Chronicle which, as mentioned, was running a series on social conditions declared, "Too few houses have been built for the working class, and too many for the middle class, hence the rents of the latter are cheaper in proportion than those of the former." Local sanitary reformers had their case strengthened in 1852 when, following the third outbreak of cholera in twenty years, a Cholera Commission of Inquiry produced a very rigourous investigation and report which concentrated on housing conditions. The Commissioners reported that "we shall not probably be over-stating the case, if we compute that about half the families in Newcastle are confined exclusively to the occupancy or joint occupancy of exceedingly over-crowded single-room tenements" (Cholera Inquiry Commission, op cit).

TABLE 2
**HOUSING CONDITIONS IN NEWCASTLE, 1866**

| **ACCOMMODATION** | | **FACILITIES** | | |
|---|---|---|---|---|
| Families in: | | Facilities | No. of Inhabitants | No. of Rooms |
| One Roomed Houses:-9639 | | No water supply | 7692 | 2594 |
| Two Roomed Houses:-6191 | | No ash pit accommodation | NA | 7206 |
| | | **Population in:** | | |
| 1 & 2 Rooms:- | 47490 (43%) | No WC or privy accommodation | 14566 | 4132 |
| 3+ Rooms:- | 62910 (57%) | None or imperfect drainage | NA | 6764 |
| | | Tenements <300 cu ft rm space | 7779 | - |
| | | Tenements <400 cu ft rm space | 18354 | - |

Source: J H Rutherford (1871)

The reports of district medical officers working for the Poor Law Guardians and census records were all confirmation of conditions which were very dangerous. In 1861 Newcastle headed the list for over-crowding in England, with 7.8 persons occupying each inhabited house. In 1866 the Public Health Committee set up under the Town Improvement Committee (Newcastle Corporation Proceedings, 1866) described the appalling conditions in the one-roomed tenements occupied by nearly 10,000 families (Table 2). The appointment of a Medical Officer of Health was forced upon the town by the Public Health Act of 1873, but the appointment was made reluctantly and against strong opposition. Alderman Gregson, himself a doctor, argued that the Medical Officer would be "a walking gentleman" and Alderman Plummer protested that the appointment "was no more use to the town than an umbrella to a duck" (ibid). Dr Henry Armstrong noted the over-crowding, high rents and insanitary conditions in his first report but the situation remained largely unchanged at the end of the century, despite a growing body of government statutes and local bye-laws which enhanced the powers of the local authority.

In a costly series of Local Improvement Acts (Gibson, 1888) Newcastle Corporation acquired various regulatory powers but, as was observed by the Cholera Commissioners and others subsequently, these powers were not always or even often exercised. It was the repeated scandal of Newcastle's position in the national death rate league at 31-32 per thousand (in St Andrew's and St Nicholas' wards it was 46 and 54), the second worst in 1866, which prompted Alderman Isaac Lothian Bell, a leading north-east industrialist, to make the first vigorous proposal in the council relevant to housing. He moved the establishment of an inquiry into the housing of the poor with a view to utilising available powers to provide working class housing (Newcastle Corporation Proceedings, 1986). Before the end of the year Newcastle's death rate had risen to first place nationally.

The investigation revealed that nearly 50,000 or 40% of Newcastle's population lived in one- or two-roomed tenements. 55,366 people lived 2.39 persons to a room. It was additionally noted that the dwellings themselves were usually situated in enclosed courts and narrow lanes which impeded ventilation; in 1,249 cases "ventilation was found scarcely to exist at all." 7,962 people had no water supply and 14,566 had no water closet or privy accommodation of any kind (Table 2). Rigid enforcement of national cubic capacity of occupancy would lead to the displacement of 7,779 individuals. But the conclusion had to be that, while many people lived in accommodation which breached sanitary legislation and which should be removed, "it cannot be done until more suitable residences have been provided for the present inmates" (Newcastle Corporation Proceedings, 1867). It was acknowledged that erecting dwellings for the working class could be done "without loss, if not with considerable financial advantage to the Corporation," but the major importance of private activity was also acknowledged. "If an effort on a small scale, commenced by the Council with their own property, could be shown to be a sound speculation, the Committee trust that an impetus would be given to private capitalists in the same direction" (ibid). It was agreed, though not without strong opposition, to adopt the Labouring Classes' Dwelling Houses Act of 1866 and the Labouring Classes and Lodging House Act of 1851, to negotiate a loan from the Public Works Commissioners and to prepare plans for working class dwellings.

The reception of the proposals provides a fine indication of social attitudes. There was much hilarity as well as some impatience in the Council meeting. Councillor Morrison asked if the proposed new block of flats was to contain a smoking room. Gregson called the whole thing "a tissue of absurdities. Four storeys? Why Charing Cross Hotel is something of that kind," and he further argued that the scheme would "take away the self-respect of the working classes" and also that the corridors envisaged in the scheme would be "nothing but scenes of clashing, idleness and smoking and one would corrupt the other." The precedent, moreover, was viewed with misgiving. "What next? Sell cheap beef to the working class; erect bakeries and also have a fleet of tailors to make cheap clothes for the working class?" Furthermore, for the Corporation to build houses and speculate was "a vicious principle" (ibid). The precise fate of the proposals is obscure, but they came to nothing. Bell himself became a director of the Industrial Dwellings Company which created tenemented dwellings at Garth Heads and this doubtless became a major preoccupation for him and a diversion from the pursuit of the Council's scheme. No one else had demonstrated similar enthusiasm.

The Public Health Act, 1875 : A Turning Point?

The 1870s saw the great Public Health Acts of 1873 and 1875 which Daunton (1984) argues marked a turning point in the regulation of house building in British cities. 1875 was also the year of the Artisans' Dwellings Act and the time when Youll took up the cause of working class housing in the Council. John Gibson Youll, a solicitor, was elected for St John's Ward in 1873 as a Liberal and was later to act as political agent for the radical Joseph Cowen. From the same year, Newcastle had a Medical Officer of Health and therefore a more regular and precise account of living conditions became available. Youll reasonably complained of "cold obstruction's apathy" (Newcastle Corporation Proceedings, 1876) after two years of pressure to produce a modest plan for the demolition of the unhealthy Pandon group of houses. He was faced with delays attributed to the "over burdening of the engineer" and, more sinister, poor attendance at Sanitary Committee meetings. When a scheme was produced in November 1876 for the purchase, demolition and erection of dwellings for 782 displaced people, Wilson, the Chairman of the Improvement Committee, assured his fellow councillors that "the Council would have nothing whatever to do with the building" (ibid). A clue to the causes of the fate of the scheme (which was abandoned after approval a year later by a Local Government Board Inquiry) perhaps can be found in the Town Clerk's warning that "there were thirty-one proprietors of the property" proposed for demolition.

## TABLE 3

## HOUSING CONDITIONS IN NEWCASTLE, 1885

**Accommodation**

| Inhabitants in: | No | % |
|---|---|---|
| One Room Tenement | 16533 | 11.3 |
| Two Room Tenement | 28181 | 19.3 |
| Other Tenements | 7322 | 5.1 |
| Self Contained Houses and Flats | 93827 | 64.3 |

**Facilities**

| Tenants in: | Tenements | | Self-Contd Houses | |
|---|---|---|---|---|
| | No | % | No | % |
| Indoor WCs | 1387 | 10.3 | 4799 | 22.8 |
| Outdoor WCs | 4919 | 36.7 | 8413 | 40.8 |
| Privies | 4795 | 35.8 | 5065 | 28.9 |
| Ash Closets | 2071 | 15.5 | 993 | 5.8 |
| Without conveniences | 157 | 1.7 | 355 | 1.6 |
| Water Supply indoors | 896 | - | 10634 | - |
| Water Supply outdoors | 3164 | _ | 8218 | - |

Source: Newcastle Council Reports (1885-86)

During the 1880s housing was rarely an issue in the Council, though a House to House Inspection by the Medical Officer of Health undertaken between 1883 and 1885 (Table 3) revealed that although 64% of the population lived in self contained houses and flats - a reversal of the 1854 situation - still a large minority of the population lived in over-crowded conditions, rents remained high and laissez-faire largely untrammelled.

On the basis of the increase in the numbers living in self-contained dwellings, it has been claimed that Newcastle's housing situation had improved considerably (Daunton, op cit, p.20). Such a claim is difficult to substantiate. Table 3 shows that 44,000 people were still living in one- or two-roomed tenements and 34.2% of the city's dwellings were in this category. In the one-room tenements there was an average of 3.1 persons per room; in the two-room tenements 2.1 and in all tenement dwellings (13,329 with 52,000 inhabitants) an average of 2.26 persons per room. In the tenement dwellings there existed 4,000 water closets (indoor and outdoor), privies and ash closets for the use of 52,000 residents. Of the 13,329 individual tenements enumerated, only 4,060 had an indoor or outdoor water supply. Of the 21,462 self-contained houses and flats, only 10,634 had an indoor water supply. At best, these figures seem to indicate that little had really changed for a large number of people between the 1860s and early 1880s and, at worst, that for many the situation had deteriorated. It is also worth noting that the intervening years - especially the 1870s - do seem to have been a period of reduced demographic pressure upon housing (see Table 1). One can only speculate on the desperate housing situation that would have ensued were it not for this hiatus.

Furthermore, it is clear from the available data that even if bye-law housing "solved the housing crisis of the middle years of the century on Tyneside" (ibid), then the solution was very short-lived. Table 4 shows the over-crowding situation in Newcastle from 1891 to 1921. In 1891 over 67,000 people were living in one- or two-roomed dwellings, testimony to the demographic pressure which built up very rapidly in the 1880s, and although this number fell slightly by 1901 it rose rapidly in the first two decades of the twentieth century. The conclusion is inescapable that, although bye-law legislation did have some impact on overall housing standards, Newcastle's housing problem remained acute throughout the whole of this period.

**TABLE 4**

**OVERCROWDING IN NEWCASTLE, 1891-1921**

| | Population | | | | Families | | | | |
|---|---|---|---|---|---|---|---|---|---|
| | In 1 Room | | In 2 Rooms | | In 1 Room | | In 2 Rooms | | % of Population |
| | No | % | No | % | No | % | No | % | over 2 per Room |
| 1891 | 15851 | 8.5 | 51607 | 27.7 | 5016 | 13.2 | 11520 | 30.4 | 32.9 |
| 1901 | 12821 | 6.0 | 51432 | 23.9 | 4249 | 9.5 | 11796 | 26.4 | 30.5 |
| 1911 | 13709 | 5.3 | 58494 | 22.8 | 4581 | 8.3 | 13087 | 23.7 | 31.6 |
| 1921 | 20866 | 7.9 | 67757 | 25.8 | 6900 | 11.5 | 15242 | 25.3 | 33.6 |

Source: Census Volumes

## The 1890s and the Impact of Working Men on the City Council

A new Housing of the Working Classes Act in 1890 simplified procedures and encouraged the supply of working class dwellings. Riley Lord was the councillor now taking the lead in housing matters. Lord was the north-east's principal representative of the Prudential Assurance Company and was councillor for the growing and predominantly working class Byker area. He led groups of councillors and officials to study working class housing in Liverpool, Edinburgh and Glasgow and gained some weighty support in the Council for his proposal to build Model Common Lodging Houses. On this occasion, the moral problems for women were argued. "It was very difficult for any woman at present to keep herself decent - driven into neighbourhoods where decency was not to be found" (Newcastle Corporation Proceedings, 1891). The proposal was for two lodging houses at the Milk Market to house 300 men and 100 women and the building of 50 one-roomed tenements at Miller's Hill. The scheme progressed at snail's pace, meeting every kind of opposition, including the spectre of the Council "getting themselves on an inclined plane which would lead them into the vortex of municipal socialism". The cost of other schemes was cited in warning. "The things were very nice and no doubt very desirable, but they were very costly...

whatever they did in that way it would mean an increase in rates." It was argued that there were plenty of rooms to let in Byker. "How was it that the Council were asked to spend all this money whilst the rate-payers who had property and were many of them dependent on the rents of their property could not get their houses let?" (ibid). We do not have a woman's voice on the subject, but it was contrarily stated by Councillor Walker both that "single women did not want to live in a room by themselves" while he asked "who were to be the few favoured women to whom they were going to let these rooms?"

By the end of 1894 the Improvement Committee "no longer recommended" proceeding with the scheme. It was later explained that, at a very poorly attended meeting, it happened that a majority of the scheme's opponents were present, but the Council also rejected the scheme by 22 votes to 8. A further discouragement was the Local Government Board's requirement of a higher standard of accommodation than that proposed for the tenement. It required at least three rooms for couples whereas the Newcastle plan, reflecting current practice for over 4,000 families in the city, suggested that one room was adequate.

The 1890s saw the entry of a small number of working men and their spokesmen into the Council. They campaigned and spoke up for a number of environment-related causes but did not promote or reflect any major campaign for housing the working class. However in 1900, at a time when many people in central Newcastle were being displaced by street and tramway works Councillor Cairns (a shipowner representing the Heaton Ward as a Liberal) took up the housing cause again and his motion for a special committee of twelve Council members and twelve citizens was accepted.

As already noted, the principal mechanism for municipal intervention in the housing system was the 1890 Housing of the Working Classes Act. This enabled municipal authorities to embark upon land purchasing and house building in addition to the replacement of houses demolished. It has been claimed that in Leeds significant improvement was achieved as the Act made compulsory purchase and compensation less expensive (Barber, 1982). Other cities used this legislation to demolish the worst of their slums and build replacement accommodation (Ashworth op cit) but Newcastle was not amongst them. A crucial factor in this legislation was the attitude of Henry Armstrong, Medical Officer of Health for the city. The housing problem was continually being debated between 1904 and 1914, due more to the pressure of the few working class representatives on the Council than to any objective appraisal of the city's housing conditions (Hunter, 1978), and it is noticeable that when Armstrong retired and was replaced by his deputy, Harold Kerr, in 1913, councillors and committee members were quickly made aware of the extent of the problem in a series of reports (Kerr, 1913). In the year before his retirement, Armstrong reported that from 1910 to 1912 only 397 dwellings were dealt with as being unfit for human habitation, and of these 174 were closed, 153 remedied and 70 were under consideration (Newcastle Corporation Proceedings, 1912). Only seven years later, Kerr reported dealing with 1845 insanitary dwellings in 1919 alone (Newcastle Corporation Proceedings, 1919).

Armstrong, however, dominated the period up to the First World War and his attitude to the housing problem is indicated in a paper he delivered in 1904 where he claimed, with justification, that the health of Newcastle's citizens was much better than it had been thirty years earlier (when he was first appointed) and, although noting the evils of over-crowding, he asked plaintively how a reduction could be brought about: "The provision, out of the rate, of dwellings for the working classes is, theoretically, fine but.... where is it to stop? At the present time there are 10,000 persons in Newcastle in need of better housing accommodation than they can afford to get for themselves. For the municipality to meet the needs of one-tenth of these and leave the rest as they are, does not look fair, does it? And how can the matter be otherwise dealt with? Life in the country should be encouraged and the urbanisation of the population discouraged in every possible way" (Armstrong, 1904). It should be noted that the 10,000 people referred to were only those living in one-room tenements, and thus fell far short of the 67,000 living in over-crowded conditions (Whitburn, 1902). Newcastle's Medical Officer of Health, who had been in some ways innovatory and energetic in matters of general health was sadly, even pathetically, at a loss when confronted with the problem of housing the working classes. Despite Armstrong's acknowledgement of the problem in his 1904 paper, it is remarkable that, in an interview with Sidney and Beatrice Webb four years earlier, he had initially strongly objected to the suggestion that Newcastle suffered from over-crowding, claiming that there were practically no cases where the bye-laws were infringed; yet later in the same interview he openly admitted that he was afraid of losing his position if he carried out his full duty, and observed that, when he had attempted to secure closing orders on over-crowded tenements in the 1890s, the magistrates - themselves property owners or close associates of such - had refused. Since then, he had attempted little (Webb, 1900).

## The Garden City Alternative

While the one man with the information available and the statutory power to initiate improvement under the 1890 Housing of the Working Classes Act refused to do so, the slow advance of working class representation on the Council, as noted above, ensured that the housing issue came to the forefront of Council affairs in the 1904-1914 period. Much of this pressure took the form of attempts to secure a garden city type of development on the Corporation-owned 800 acre Walker Estate. John Whitburn, councillor for Elswick South, an ILP member, and the Newcastle Trades Council president, had first raised the issue in Council debate in 1901 (Newcastle Corporation Proceedings, 1902) and further publicised the suggestion a year later in his booklet "The Housing Problem in Newcastle and District" (Whitburn, op cit). In the same year a letter from a local churchman, Rev. T D Landels, MA, strongly urged the Council to undertake the building of "a municipal Bourneville" at Walker (Newcastle Corporation Proceedings, 1902) and in December 1903 a petition from 2,500 rate-payers was introduced, requesting that the Council initiate a garden city type of development (ibid, 1904). Four years later a mass meeting of workers was held at the Elswick Works of W G Armstrong and Co and a petition on the same subject sent to the newly-formed Housing of the Poor sub-committee (Housing of the Poor Sub-Committee Minutes, 1907).

The establishment of this sub-committee represented at least a partial victory for the housing lobby, but the principal objective remained the building of a garden city on the outskirts of Newcastle. Enthusiasm for the project had increased after some Council members had visited the National Housing Reform Conference at Letchworth in 1905. The main proponent became David Adams, elected to represent All Saints North Ward for Labour in 1902, who persuaded the Council to act as hosts for a further Garden City Conference in Newcastle. Part of the Walker Estate was to be used for the purpose and the Corporation agreed to build twelve model cottages at Walkerville as their contribution to the Exhibition. The remainder - 68 - were to be built by private builders as entries for a design competition (Walkergate Model Cottages Exhibition, 1908). In 1908, Adams published a monograph urging much larger-scale developments on garden city lines and, with acknowledgements to Raymond Unwin, included plans of suggested lay-outs and sketches of house types. He claimed that a population of 48,000 could be housed, providing an annual income from ground rents above £200,000 (Adams, 1908).

Thus, for most of the 1904-1914 period the focus of debate was the future development of the large Corporation property of the Walker Estate. In some respects, this unintentionally diverted attention away from worsening housing conditions for a large number of people in Newcastle. In particular, it distracted attention from the links between the housing problem and poverty and insecure employment. The concentration on how the Walker Estate could best be developed produced a dichotomy within the Council between a minority urging large-scale municipal house building and the majority arguing that the practical difficulties of developing the Estate were overwhelming and that, in any case, the solution to the housing problem was best left in the hands of private enterprise.

## Problems and Progress 1906-1914

Some municipal developments in working class housing were taking place in Newcastle, however, but by March 1917 only 455 tenement dwellings had been provided in six small schemes (Housing of the Poor Sub- Committee Minutes, 1917). The first municipal dwellings, at Walker Road and Albion Row were, strictly speaking, Displaced Labourers' Dwellings, built in 1904 for people displaced by tramway development. Most of the early schemes took the form of single-room tenements but even with this modest type of development concern over costs delayed progress. The predominant attitude to municipal involvement in the housing field can be seen in the views expressed by people like Henry Armstrong who suggested cutting costs by building temporary dwellings of flimsier materials (ibid, 1906) and in July 1906 the proposed rents for a group of single-roomed tenements were reduced from 4s.3d. per week to 3s.8d. by reducing the area of building and the number of water closets, giving one to be shared by four apartments (ibid). In March 1906, in the largest municipal development to be attempted before the First World War, 126 tenements at the Newton Road and St Lawrence Road development were completed, but when the Housing of the Poor Sub-committee attempted to hand them over to the Estates and Property Committee for their management, the latter refused to accept them. Such lack of sympathy between the various committees of the Council was a prominent feature of this period and added considerably to the problems of progressing towards an adequate, co-ordinated policy for municipal housing. Even in the more optimistic circumstances towards the end of the war the lack of co-operation between relevant committees remained a problem. The Housing Committee planned to make 116 acres of the Walker Estate available for housing immediately after the war, but the Chairman of the notoriously conservative Estates and Property Committee (which controlled the Walker Estate) objected and suggested that 50 acres would be sufficient land to deal with at one time (ibid, 1918).

At the same time, it seems clear that relatively high rents coupled with suspicion at the degree of supervision, delayed the full occupancy of Council dwellings. Even when housing was provided, the Council had problems in managing it effectively. One year after their opening, 55 of the 126 tenements at Newton Dwellings and St Lawrence Road were un-let and in September 1907 the conditions of tenancy were made "less irksome" and in February 1908 rent reductions took place (ibid, 1908).

**TABLE 5**

**NEWCASTLE UPON TYNE CITY COUNCIL: ATTENDANCE AT COMMITTEES**

| Committee | Total Meetings | Actual | Attendance Possible | % |
|---|---|---|---|---|
| 1906/7 | | | | |
| Full Council | 27 | 1638 | 2052 | 79.8 |
| Finance | 26 | 474 | 728 | 65.1 |
| Town Improvement | 71 | 1315 | 2201 | 59.3 |
| Sanitary | 35 | 617 | 1085 | 56.9 |
| Estate and Property | 22 | 356 | 638 | 55.8 |
| Housing | 15 | 330 | 615 | 53.6 |
| 1911/12 | | | | |
| Full Council | 16 | 947 | 1216 | 77.9 |
| Finance | 19 | 324 | 513 | 63.2 |
| Town Improvement | 64 | 988 | 1472 | 67.1 |
| Sanitary | 26 | 400 | 650 | 61.5 |
| Estate and Property | 24 | 350 | 600 | 58.3 |
| Housing | 13 | 128 | 221 | 57.9 |
| 1920/21 | | | | |
| Full Council | 18 | 1033 | 1368 | 75.5 |
| Finance | 31 | 454 | 868 | 52.3 |
| Town Improvement | 38 | 523 | 988 | 52.9 |
| Sanitary | 25 | 311 | 650 | 47.8 |
| Estate and Property | 15 | 210 | 360 | 58.3 |
| Housing | 32 | 393 | 992 | 39.6 |

Source: Newcastle Council Reports

The lack of commitment to meaningful Council intervention in housing in this period is apparent in the low attendance of councillors at the sub-committee meetings compared to other committees and the main Council (Table 5). Even more revealing is the fact that the Housing of the Poor sub-committee was disbanded between November 1909 and November 1911, all housing matters being dealt with by the Sanitary Committee. Interestingly enough, this period coincided almost exactly with a period of reversals in the election of working class representatives to Newcastle City Council (Hunter, op cit). For a vital two years, therefore, the focus of the housing issue became diffused yet again and the debate was deflected away from the provision of housing per se onto the related but less politically sensitive sanitary and health issues.

It is clear that, along with the rest of North East England, Newcastle was notorious for its poor housing conditions yet, in contrast to cities such as Liverpool, Glasgow and London and probably also Birmingham, Leeds, Manchester and Sheffield, little was done either in terms of building municipal property or in the other forms of remedial intervention available, especially slum clearance. Major obstacles to the latter were the property interests on the council together with the unfavourable ratio of wages to rents for manual labourers. Both factors militated against any significant municipal involvement in slum clearance before the First World War. Many working class dwellings were in fact cleared in the last few decades of the nineteenth century and the first decade of the twentieth century but commercial redevelopment and transport improvements were largely responsible. It has been claimed that as many as 5,000 dwellings were lost in the inner parts of Newcastle by this process at this time (Meacham, 1977) and between 1908 and 1919, 900 dwellings were officially recorded as being lost to commercial development (Medical Officer of Health's Reports, 1908-1919). Inevitably, most of these were the centrally-located heavily sub-divided tenements which traditionally provided accommodation for the unskilled and semi-skilled workers, especially those in 'casualised' industries. Such families were therefore squeezed between a diminishing amount of cheap, centrally-located accommodation and the extreme reluctance of the local authority to provide any alternative. In addition, it must be stressed that much of this property was insanitary and subject to high levels of overcrowding. For example, a survey in 1884 found 230 families in 50 houses in Blandford Street, 140 families with 34 houses in Blenheim Street and 310 families in 62 houses in George Street (Royal Commission on the Housing of the Working Classes, 1884 - evidence of Rev. W E Handley). Yet, the shortage of replacement dwellings increased the reluctance of the authorities to fully carry out both local and national public health legislation - 'Why demolish properties in the name of slum clearance when there was nowhere for the displaced tenants to go?' - was a frequent question in the Council Chamber.

**TABLE 6**

**NEWCASTLE UPON TYNE COUNCIL: OCCUPATIONAL STRUCTURE, 1881-1921**

| **Occupation** | **1881** | **1901** | **1921** |
|---|---|---|---|
| Legal Profession | 9.4 | 4.7 | 3.9 |
| Other Professions | 10.9 | 20.3 | 18.4 |
| Retail Trade | 32.8 | 29.7 | 31.6 |
| Merchants/Shipping | 25.0 | 25.0 | 15.8 |
| Manufacturing Industry | 9.4 | 4.7 | 3.9 |
| Direct Property Interests | 10.9 | 12.5 | 7.9 |
| Others | 1.6 | 1.6 | 7.9 |
| Working Men | - | 1.6 | 7.9 |
| Not Known | - | - | 3.9 |
| | N=64 | N=64 | N=76 |

Source: Newcastle Council Reports: City Directories

There is no doubt that commercial interests dominated Newcastle City Council throughout this period (Table 6) and whilst it is less easy to trace those with direct or indirect property interests on the Council, it seems likely from Table 6 that they were well represented and a number of examples have been cited elsewhere (Benwell Community Development Report, 1978). It was certainly the case in the 1880s that "... individual members of the corporation are owners of tenement property and it is not, I am bound to say, in the best condition." (Minutes of Evidence, Royal Commission on the Housing of the Working Classes, October 1884). Negative attitudes to municipal involvement to house provision should therefore not surprise us, neither should a similar view of any form of interference in the housing market, even if it took the form of sanitary improvement (Webb, 1900). As late as 1913 the Clerk to the Poor Law Guardians of the Newcastle upon Tyne Union could observe: "In Newcastle ... the Corporation have not put into force that part of the (1890) Housing Act which permits the dealing with areas for improvement or demolition of labouring class houses. And their Local Act is insufficient for the purpose in hand." (Walker, 1914). Thus, both municipal building and clearance of working class dwellings were either negligible or limited, although the operation of the property market produced a substantial amount of the latter. Circumstantial evidence suggests that the property interests of a large proportion of the City Council would make them ill-disposed towards any form of local authority involvement in housing and even if not directly involved in property, the ideological position of many more ensured that they shared this view.

When housing issues were raised in Council debates, a common question asked by those opposed to municipal intervention was - why, if there is such a shortage of decent housing, are there so many vacant dwellings in the city? Vacant dwellings did indeed exist. For example, in November 1912 it was estimated that there were 306 empty self-contained houses and 930 empty flats within the city (Housing of the Poor Sub-Committee Minutes, February 1913). However, we are not told the rentals of these properties or their location and by February 1914 there were only 387 vacant dwellings (Newcastle Corporation Proceedings, 1913-14). There is no doubt that the major demand for housing for the majority of the unskilled and semi-skilled working classes was in and around the city centre, related to potential sources of employment. A special inquiry in the Quayside area in 1913 found 3207 inhabited dwellings ".. occupied almost entirely by the casual labourer class, chiefly Quayside workers, together with hawkers etc, the average wage being 18/- per week". (Kerr, 1913). Furthermore, that demand was also for accommodation at affordable rents. Yet Whitburn comments (1902): "There are many instances in this City wherein not less than one quarter and in some cases one third of the total income has to be applied (in rent)," and cites examples of labourers earning between 18/- and 23/- per week paying rents of 5/6d to 7/- per week. He goes on to note that "It has often been remarked by employers that it was useless giving the men an advance of wages because rents were immediately raised to about the same extent." (op cit p.20). A decade later, the persistence of Whitburn's assertions are shown - both by Kerr's 1913 report on the Quayside (op cit) and a further investigation - ".. in very few places can the poor escape with the payment of less than one fourth of their earnings in rent." (Walker, 1914, p.4). Table 7 confirms that housing in Newcastle (and the north-east generally) was an expensive commodity for working class families compared to many other places and it should be noted that the city and region generally lacked the opportunities for female employment available elsewhere, employment which could supplement the total household income. Against this background it seems reasonable to conclude that if property was vacant at a time of otherwise apparently high pressure on housing, it was because it was either in unsuitable locations or too expensive.

**TABLE 7**

**WAGES AND RENT LEVELS IN ENGLISH CITIES, 1905**

| | Rent Index | Wage index | Ratio of wages |
|---|---|---|---|
| London | 100 | 100 | 1.0 |
| Subdivided property | | | |
| Plymouth & Devonport | 81 | 80 | 1.0 |
| Tyneside flats | | | |
| Newcastle | 76 | 90 | 1.2 |
| Gateshead | 66 | 90 | 1.4 |
| South Shields | 61 | 88 | 1.5 |
| Single-storey cottages | | | |
| Sunderland | 59 | 88 | 1.5 |
| Back-to-backs | | | |
| Bradford | 59 | 83 | 1.4 |
| Halifax | 55 | 82 | 1.5 |
| Leeds | 56 | 87 | 1.6 |
| Lancashire: through houses without back additions | | | |
| Oldham | 60 | 92 | 1.5 |
| Burnley | 53 | 85 | 1.6 |
| Bolton | 53 | 90 | 1.7 |
| Blackburn | 50 | 87 | 1.7 |
| Midlands and South: through houses with back additions | | | |
| Cardiff | 59 | 92 | 1.6 |
| Nottingham | 56 | 92 | 1.6 |
| Birmingham | 59 | 98 | 1.7 |
| Bristol | 53 | 93 | 1.8 |
| Ipswich | 44 | 86 | 2.0 |
| Leicester | 48 | 94 | 2.0 |

Source: PP 1908 CVIII, Report of an Enquiry by the Board of Trade into working-class rents, housing and retail prices, tables E, ppl-li.

By the second decade of the twentieth century, however, a greater urgency began to enter the proceedings of the Council and its committees in relation to housing. For example, in October 1912 the Council at last agreed to proceed with a Housing Scheme on the Walker Estate (Housing of the Poor Sub-Committee Minutes, 1912). In part this was prompted by the example set by a reforming central government, but also significant was the shock of the 1911 census with its revelations about the state of housing, especially overcrowding, in Newcastle compared with other large cities (ibid, 1913). Furthermore, the rapid decline in private sector house-building was producing a still worse housing situation in the city (Benwell Community Project, 1978). By May 1913, a search for suitable housing sites was under way, albeit with a degree of weary resignation on the part of those charged with the task: "In accordance with the instructions of this Committee.....that the Property Surveyor suggest suitable sites for the west and central portions of the City for Municipal Dwellings, the Surveyor reports that a similar instruction was given to him on 27th November 1905.....and the Surveyor herewith re-submits the sketch plans of the sites then inspected" (Housing of the Poor Sub-Committee Minutes, 1913). Nothing could give clearer testimony to the funereal rate of progress with regard to municipal involvement in housing.

Yet it is the case that, however late, immediately before the First World War, some action was being taken and three schemes were in preparation: 123 dwellings at St Lawrence Square; 44 at Sallyport Crescent and 402 in Walker. Nonetheless, pressure was mounting on the Council from all sides. The severe shortage of houses was creating new slum conditions where none had existed before, commercial development was reducing the amount of residential accommodation in the central area, and at the same time substantial areas of insanitary property remained to be dealt with. These pressures were exacerbated by the enforced delay in house construction brought on with the outbreak of war. One cannot escape the conclusion that the inactivity of the previous several decades meant that Newcastle was to be faced with continuing massive housing problems for many decades to come.

## Conclusion

Newcastle upon Tyne remained notorious for its over-crowding and high death rate throughout the period with which we are concerned. This chapter has explored the constraints which militated against any significant intervention by the municipal authority to deal with such problems. Such inertia persisted despite a series of scandals, revelations, and moves by local pressure groups and councillors. The constraints upon positive action range across the prevailing ideology of self-help, the uncertainty about responsibility, the reluctance of a Council dominated by business-men to increase their own rates and the rates of those who elected them, a lack of confidence in Council competence, the anxiety of significant officials such as the Medical Officer of Health and the Borough Engineer about the security of their positions, and procedural inadequacies in the Council generally and in particular certain committees and sub-committees. Issues other than housing predominated until the twentieth century, when the pressure of working men councillors, who entered the Council from the 1890s, brought housing to the forefront of Council business at a period when enthusiasm for landlordism was declining. Yet, even in such a changing climate of opinion prevarication continued. Whilst more councillors now agreed that something ought to be done there was little unanimity over the precise form of intervention. Even the fact that the Council itself owned a substantial amount of underdeveloped land in the form of the Walker Estate did not significantly ease the path of municipal intervention.

**Michael Barke**
**Maureen Callcott**

**PLATE 1**
Appletree Gardens, Walkerville. Walkerville Garden City Scheme.
Note the For Sale signs in this 1912 photograph.

**PLATE 2**
Garth Heads Tenements.
Newcastle's only pre 1914 working class flatted development.

**PLATE 3**
Sallyport Crescent.
An early example of municipal housing in Newcastle.

## References


Adams, D. (1908) The Planning and Development of Walker and Willington Estates, Newcastle upon Tyne Labour Representation Committee.

Allen, C.M. (1965) The genesis of British urban redevelopment with special reference to Glasgow, Economic History Review, 2nd series, Vol. 18, 598-613.

Armstrong, H.G. (1904) The Supposed Deterioration and Decrease of our Population in Relation to Over-crowding in Houses, Paper read before the Diocesan Conference in Newcastle upon Tyne, October 4.

Ashworth, W. (1954) The Genesis of Modern British Town Planning London. Routledge and Kegan Paul.

Barber, R. (1982) Municipal government in Leeds, in Fraser, D. (ed). Municipal Reform and the Industrial City Leicester: Leicester University Press.

Barke, M. and Buswell, R.J. (1980) Historical Atlas of Newcastle upon Tyne Newcastle upon Tyne: Petras.

Benwell Community Project (1978) Private Housing and the Working Class Final Report Series Newcastle upon Tyne.

Briggs, A. (1952) History of Birmingham, Vol.2, Borough and City, 1865-1938 London: Oxford University Press.

The Builder (1861), 13 April.

Cholera Inquiry Commission (1854), Minutes of Evidence, Newcastle upon Tyne.

Daunton, M.J. (1984) House and Home in the Victorian City: Working Class Housing, 1850-1914 London: Edward Arnold.

Gaskell, S.M. (1976) Sheffield City Council and the development of suburban areas prior to World War I in Pollard, S. and Holmes, C. (eds). Essays in the Economic and Social History of South Yorkshire Barnsley: South Yorkshire County Council, 187-202.

Gouldie, E. (1974) Cruel Habitations: A History of Working-Class Housing, 1780-1918 London: Allen and Unwin.

Gibson, J.F. (1888) Newcastle upon Tyne Acts and Bye-Laws, 1837-1877 Newcastle upon Tyne.

Harrison, M. (1981) Housing and town planning in Manchester before 1914 in Sutcliffe, A. (ed). British Town Planning, the Formative Years Leicester: Leicester University Press, 64-105.

Housing of the Poor Sub-Committee Minutes, Newcastle Corporation, 1906, 1907, 1908, 1912, 1913, 1918.

Hunter, I.G. (1978) Working Class Representation in Elective Local Authorities on Tyneside, 1883-1921. Unpublished M. Litt. thesis, Newcastle University.

Kerr, H. (1913) Housing in the Quayside Area. Report of Special Inquiry Newcastle upon Tyne: Newcastle Housing Committee and Sanitary Committee

Newcastle Corporation Proceedings, 1848, 1866, 1867, 1876, 1891, 1902.

Meacham, S. (1977) A Life Apart - the English Working Class, 1890-1914, London, Thames and Hudson.

Pooley, C.G. (1985) Housing for the poorest poor: slum clearance and rehousing in Liverpool, 1890-1918 Journal of Historical Geography Vol.11, No.1, 70-88.

P.R.O. MH13/323 (1848) Letter from Charleton Baynes to Edwin Chadwick, 17th October.

Rawlinson, R. (1853) Report to the General Board of Health, 1853 P.R.O. MH13/232.

Reid, D.R. (1845) Report on the State of Newcastle upon Tyne and Other Large Towns

Rowe, D.J. (1977) Population of nineteenth-century Tyneside in McCord, N. (ed). Essays in Tyneside Labour History Newcastle upon Tyne: Department of Humanities, Newcastle Polytechnic.

Rutherford, J.H. (1871) The public health of Newcastle upon Tyne in 1866 and 1869 in Pears, E. (ed) Transactions of the National Association for the Promotion of Social Science, London.

Smith, P.J. (1980) Planning as environmental improvement: slum clearance in Edinburgh in Sutcliffe, A. (ed). The Rise of Modern Urban Planning 1800-1914 London: Mansell, 99-134.

Smith, R., Whysall, P., and Beuvrin, C. (1986) Local authority inertia in housing improvement 1890-1914 Town Planning Review, Vol.57, No.4, 404-424.

Taylor, I.C. (1974) The insanitary housing question and tenement dwellings in nineteenth century Liverpool in Sutcliffe, A. (ed). Multi-Storey Living London: Croom Helm, 88-121.

Walker, G. (1914) The Housing Problem in its Relation to Disease and the Poor Rate in Newcastle upon Tyne. Ms. held in Local History Library, Newcastle upon Tyne City Library.

Walkergate Model Cottages Exhibition, Catalogue (1908).

Webb, S. (1900) Local Government Collection, Vol.217. Ms. British Library of Political and Economic Science.

Whitburn, J. (1902) The Housing Problem in Newcastle and District Newcastle upon Tyne: W. H. Robinson.

Yelling, J.A. (1981) The selection of sites for slum clearance in London, 1875-1888 Journal of Historical Geography, Vol.7, No.2, 155-165.

# NEWCASTLE'S TYNESIDE FLATS 1850-1900
# BY-LAW HOUSING OR CULTURAL PHENOMENON?

## Introduction

Historians of working class housing have long puzzled over the origins and regional dominance of the 'Tyneside flat'. Although the 'cottage flat' is also found elsewhere, nowhere else did it ever assume the Tyneside form or the same acceptance. The 1911 census of England and Wales reveals that only 2.9% of the population lived in flats. Yet in Northumberland and County Durham the percentage was 25.4% and 14.6% respectively. And in Newcastle it was 55.67%, Gateshead 62.5% and South Shields 63.1%. (1) Moreover, according to M J Daunton they were only the prevalent house-type in a narrow five mile band on each side of the River Tyne. (2)

There have been many attempts to explain their origins and evolution, with various speculative theories. However, at best these are only secondary factors, and therefore will only be briefly considered. Instead greater emphasis will be given to their historical context, innate qualities of design, the effect of local building regulations and economic and cultural factors. Nevertheless, theories of the origins and evolution of Tyneside flats are germane to any attempted explanation of their peculiar dominance in Tyneside. But these approaches presuppose that the subsequent dominance of Tyneside flats was inevitable. An evolving form pre-supposes that the most popular house-type must be that best suited to the environment. Although a plausible deduction it depends too heavily on notions of 'process', 'development' and 'evolution'. The effect is to exaggerate impersonal 'forces' and to minimise human agency and choice, revealing reductionism dressed up as plausible explanations.

For instance, Anthony Sutcliffe constantly refers to the combined effect of pre-industrial traditions of urban housing and "the habitual conservatism" of builders and investors that perpetuated traditional housing during the process of urbanisation. (3) He also argues that the political independence of European cities and constant warfare made defensive walls necessary long after most British towns had demolished theirs and that the walls were 'the over-riding restriction' which predisposed towns in most of Europe towards higher buildings'. (4) This is meant to explain why no national tradition of flat dwellings arose in Britain. Since Newcastle demolished its walls far later than most other English cities, its similarity with the European experience is meant to explain the peculiar dominance of Tyneside flats.
He supports his theory by referring to "certain natural obstacles" in Newcastle. (5) Restrictions on expansion were caused by the refusal of Newcastle's Freemen to allow expansion onto the Town Moor; a large area of central Newcastle undeveloped until 1835, and then primarily as a commercial development; and the deep ravines of tributaries of the Tyne that created natural barriers to the east and west until the early nineteenth century.

Such theories have a certain plausibility, but they rely too heavily on suppositions, one of which is that Newcastle is the birth place of Tyneside flats. Furthermore, York still has its town walls and both Liverpool and Sheffield occupy steep riverside sites, and yet none developed a similar dominant housing form. Clearly the Tyneside flat must be explained by more than a speculative theory about the effect of restricted expansion in the early stages of urbanisation.

Stefan Muthesius argues that Tyneside flats 'evolved' from early house-types and traces elements of the 'mature

Tyneside flat' (as it were) to late eighteenth century forerunners. He implicitly claims that the isolated example of an old type of alms-house, built in 1796 at Heddon-on-the-Wall as miners homes, must be an 'ancestor' of the Tyneside flat. (6) He argues that four basic similarities shared by 'Sunderland cottages' and Tyneside flats are sufficient proof of the evolution of the latter, and he and Sutcliffe claim that the proximity of similar 'Scottish flats' may have been an example from which Tyneside flats developed. (7)

However, Muthesius overlooks the fact that Sunderland cottages were contemporary, not earlier house-types. Indeed he describes them as "a blend of colliery housing and Sunderland bye-laws" which dates them at about the 1860's - like Tyneside flats. (8) His reference to Scottish flats is probably to some built at Rosebank, Edinburgh in 1857. Muthesius confuses his argument by mixing two speculative developmental theories. First that Tyneside flats are an indigenous form, the product of steep banks, creating a tradition from which Tyneside flats later evolved. And yet other towns on similar sites failed to develop a similar house-type. Furthermore, it relies on the unproven assumption that Newcastle is the source of the form. His theory is an unverified belief in a form of natural selection, and is therefore unhistorical. His second theory is that Tyneside flats were based upon examples beyond Tyneside. Both the alms-house in Heddon-on-the-Wall and Sunderland cottages fit into this argument, even though they are 'local', and the example, of the Scottish flats is clearer still. However, he seems to be totally unaware that these were model cottages, specifically designed as examples to be copied and adapted. Furthermore, these are pre-dated by model housing built in 1846 in London (far earlier than any examples of Tyneside flats I have been able to find in Newcastle), and described by J N Tarn as 'cottage flats'. (9)

Muthesius wants it both ways: to argue that Tyneside flats were an indigenous house-type and yet based on examples from beyond Tyneside. Although in a very limited sense this is plausible the first argument is seriously undermined by the second.

The value of Muthesius' theories is that one of these is united to a sophisticated explanation given by M J Daunton, who builds on the former's undeveloped theory that local bye-law regulations were crucial in allowing Tyneside flats to become the dominant working-class house type. Daunton claims that:

> "the bye-laws institutionalised an earlier form of housing which had developed as a pragmatic response to the division of property in the old, densely populated central area [of Newcastle] in the mid-nineteenth century." (10)

He constructs a complex network of causal factors, the convergence of which purport to explain the dominance of Tyneside flats from the 1870's, and so far it is the most satisfactory explanation.

This chapter will use Daunton's sophisticated explanation, whilst subjecting its assumption and conclusions to close scrutiny. The first part considers the history of Newcastle's housing problem in the national context of the nineteenth century. From the perspective of the architectural historian the second emphasises the simplicity, versatility and cheapness of the design of Tyneside flats, and cursively comments on the pretensions of their middle class facade. In the third section M J Daunton's theory that bye-law building regulations institutionalised the Tyneside flat by discouraging the construction of tenements will be closely examined, by briefly identifying those elements regulated by local bye-laws, and by considering the probable motives for such regulations. The last section will assess the economic attractions of Tyneside flats for all concerned. It will also supplement such factors with others which I have called "the social acceptability" of Tyneside flats, linking economic, social and cultural factors relating to the role of land owners, speculators, landlords and the local council, as well as a consideration of the social value placed on Tyneside flats as a form of social control over Tyneside flat dwellers. This work concentrates on Newcastle because limited time prevented wider research. Even if Newcastle is not the source of their form it is the ideal focus of such a study because of the large numbers and variety of those built, plus well documented details of its bye-laws and many other valuable sources.

## The History of Newcastle's Housing Problem

Figure A shows that the population of England and Wales doubled between 1801 and 1851, and did so again by 1911. Such statistics go a long way to explaining the severity of the housing problem in nineteenth century cities.

Figure A.

| Population of England and Wales | |
|---|---|
| 1801 | c9m. |
| 1851 | 17.9m |
| 1871 | 22.7m. |
| 1891 | 29m. |
| 1911 | 36.07m. |

The rising population, accompanied by immigration and rural emigration to towns, manifested itself in growing urbanisation. John Burnett writes that:

> "In 1801 probably around 80% of the population of England and Wales was still 'rural' and only some 20% 'urban', defined as living in towns having more than 5,000 inhabitants". (11)

Yet within fifty years 54% of the people lived in 'urban' areas as against 46% in 'rural' areas. As the century advanced this trend was clearly seen in rapidly growing towns illustrated in Figure B, which shows a five-fold population increase between 1831 and 1911 in Newcastle, and the even more spectacular growth of Middlesborough.

Figure B

| Urban Growth | 1801 | to | 1911 |
|---|---|---|---|
| London | 1.75m | | 4.5m |
| York | 26,000 | | 78,000 |
| Birmingham | 144,000 | | 500,000 |
| Manchester | 182,000 | | 544,000 |
| Liverpool | 202,000 | | 685,000 |
| Middlesborough | 154 | | 91,000 |
| Newcastle upon Tyne | 53,613 | | 271,523 |

12

Figure C is a graph of the comparative growth of Tyneside's four main towns which shows how much larger and more rapid was Newcastle's urbanisation than its neighbours. The density and rapidity of its urbanisation was a crucial factor in the development of Tyneside flats.

# FIGURE C

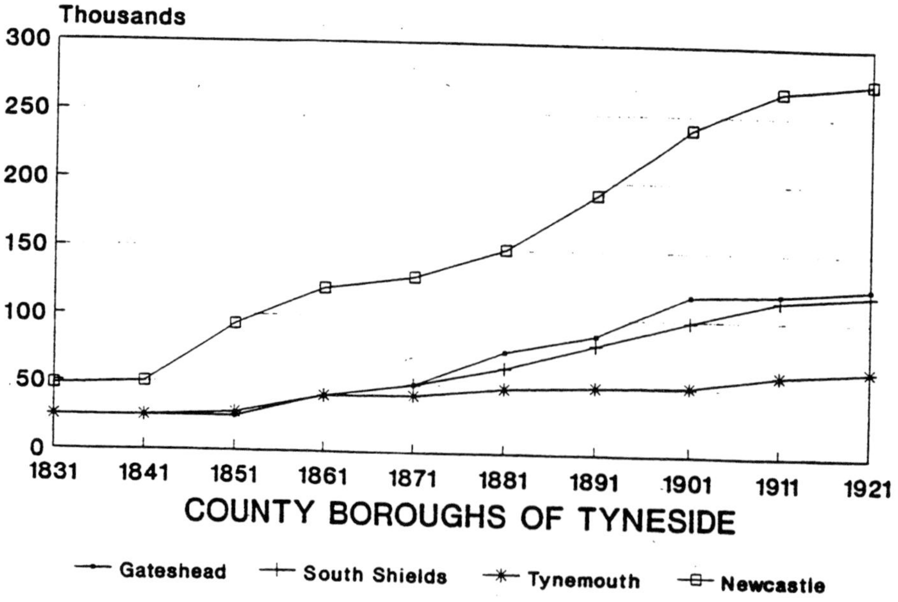


The four Country Borough of Tyneside: comparative populations [13]

The sustained population growth between 1831 and 1921 is given in greater detail in Figure D, which shows the comparative growth of Newcastle's suburbs. It shows that from 1831 to 1871 Westage, Elswick and Byker grew rapidly in size, and that Heaton, Benwell and Jesmond followed suit from 1881 to 1891. The most spectacular rises are in Elswick and Byker, both are areas where large numbers of Tyneside flats were built. The former reflects the presence of Armstrong's Elswick Works, founded in 1847 and employing about 25,000 men by 1900.(14) In the 1880's Heaton and Benwell also had large numbers of Tyneside flats built.

# FIGURE D

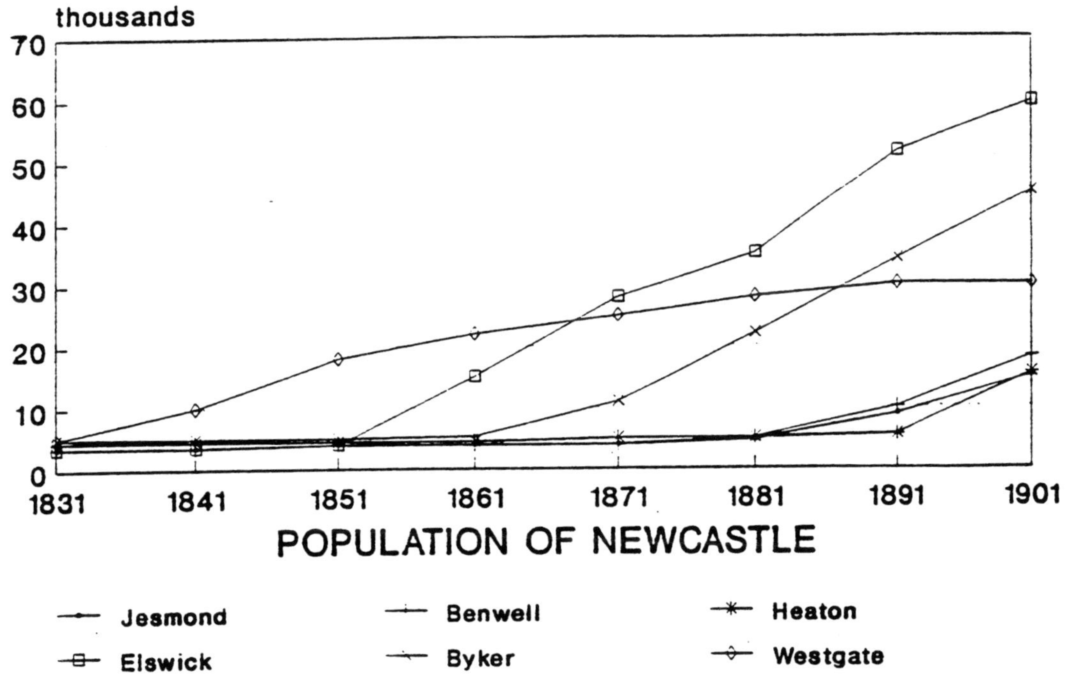


Comparative growth of population in the suburbs of Newcastle[15]

The spectacular expansion of Armstrong's from the 1850's illustrates the large numbers of people attracted to Newcastle's many thriving industries. Between 1863 and 1883 the workforce of Stephenson Hawthorn, in Forth Banks, rose from 6,000 to 20,000.[16] These spectacular increases in the working population were also evident in numerous local collieries, smaller engineering firms and other factories making glass, rope, chemicals, pottery and so forth. By 1878 Maling's potteries in Byker employed nearly 1,000 men.[17] In addition thousands of casual workers were based at the Quayside, and growing numbers worked in the commercial and retail trade of Newcastle's growing town centre. It has been called "the swiftest and most remarkable period of industrial expansion in the whole history of the northern coalfield."[18] Overcrowding was the result of such rapid expansion. As elsewhere the oldest parts of town become the most densely populated areas. Large houses, formerly owned by merchants who had since moved to less populous, healthier suburbs, were converted into grossly overcrowded tenements.

The 1866 Report of Public Health graphically illustrates the extent of overcrowding by showing how many people lived in a house, and the percentage of families who lived in just one or two rooms. Even though there is some doubt how reliable such official figures were in the nineteenth century, they allow valuable comparisons. for instance, the report shows that in 1851, 87,184 persons lived in 10,441 houses (or 8.3 persons per house), and that in 1861 109,108 lived in 13,979 houses (or 7.8 per house). The latter figure was higher than the nine other cities used for comparison. And only London, Liverpool and Bristol had more than 5 persons per house.

The 1854 Cholera Commission reported that nearly 35% of families lived in self-contained houses and 65.3% in tenements. Of the latter 23.5% lived in two rooms and

39.3% in just one room![19] Even though there had been some improvement by 1866, 43% of the townspeople still lived in one or two rooms. H A Mess argued that this helps to explain why Tyneside flats wee seen as a solution: The working population were used to one or two rooms of squalor, and therefore two or three rooms of better, self-contained housing was a real improvement.[20] However, although a plausible explanation of market demand, it does not explain why Tyneside flats were built when elsewhere, in similar urban conditions, tenements or terraced housing was built instead.

At the beginning of the second half of the nineteenth century Newcastle clearly had some of the worst urban problems in the whole country. These problems, linked with the spectacular population increase, are important - though unquantifiable - factors in the acceptance of Tyneside flats as a solution to Newcastle's housing problem. However, they need to be placed in the context of political and philanthropic initiatives at the national and local level.
The reaction to government legislation can be seen from the comments of Robert Plummer, who gave evidence to the 1840 Sanitary Inquiry. Whilst agreeing that building regulations were needed, he feared that legislation would be construed as "uncalled for interference with private property, speculation and emolument". As early as 1853 the Report of the Sanitary Committee to the council argued that to solve the housing problem "An example ought to be set by the Corporation or by individuals, in constructing Houses for Habitation of the humbler classes". By 1866 Newcastle's Medical Officer of Health was even more forthright in a Council debate:

> "Private enterprise does not step in and afford the necessary shelter (for the labouring classes). Besides, supposing that that were so, you cannot compel private landlords to undertake duties which belong more closely to the Corporation itself".[21]

There were many dissenting voices; councillors arguing variously that self help was the proper answer, or that merely setting an example was the limit to the Corporation's role, or even that private enterprise could have coped if excessive rates on tenements had not made them an unprofitable solution.[22]

Given the evident resistance to government initiatives, it becomes clear why philanthropists formed themselves into societies and charities in the hope that 'model housing' would encourage private enterprise to provide adequate housing. An early example was The Society for Improving the Conditions of the Labouring Classes, formed in 1844 and supported by such luminaries as Lord Shaftesbury and the Prince Consort. In 1846 its first model housing scheme included a few two-storey houses of flats.[23] Although most societies promoted tenements or lodging houses as the best form of model housing for the working classes, there were other highly acclaimed proposals.

The most important for our study was that of model worker's cottages championed by the Prince of Wales. His own fame gave great publicity to the pretty Alexandra Cottages which he had built on his Sandringham estate.[24] In a lengthy letter addressed to Newcastle's mayor called "Sandringham : Its Lessons", Nicholas Gibson ('a deputy landlord') proposed a more economically viable and socially acceptable compromise. He states that he agrees with the verdict of the Duchess of Lothair, "you must take care that your cottages are not villas".[25] Not for the first time in Newcastle, he argued that the local industrialists should build workmen's cottages near their factories. As early as 1854 the Newcastle Temperance Society had proposed the same solution, and were naturally keen that such developments should improve the inhabitants morals as well as their health.[26]

We need to note that by 1885 the pattern of housing conditions had radically changed. In 1854 34.7% of Newcastle's families lived in self-contained houses and 65.3% in tenements. Now 64.3% of the population lived in self-contained houses and flats and 35.7% in tenements - a reversal of the earlier pattern. It was the construction of large numbers of Tyneside flats which had effected this change. The remainder of this essay will try to explain why this house-type became predominant in Newcastle.

## The Design of Tyneside Flats

The design of Tyneside flats clearly contributed to their popularity. For a variety of reasons they had an appeal for builders, landlords and occupiers. However, for our purpose it is only necessary to briefly remark on the inherent qualities of their terraced form, individual facade and internal layout. In doing so the contrasts between their external appearance and their very basic interior will become evident.

There were two basic varieties: the two-room flat on the ground floor with a three-room flat above, reputedly built from as early as 1845, but I have been unable to substantiate this. The earliest plans that I could find for such flats were dated 1862 and built in Elswick, but there were undoubtedly many built earlier.[27]

The second variety was the three-room ground floor flat with a four-room flat above. There are examples from the 1870's, but it was not until the 1880's that they became prevalent variety.[28] However, even then the older, cheaper and more basic variety continued to be built.[29] Generally there was very little difference in the basic design of the two varieties.

## The Terraced Form

The architectural unity of a terrace of Tyneside flats often disguises the fact that it may contain a mixture of flats and houses, similarly it may easily absorb a corner shop. Such variations reveal the essential simplicity and versatility of their terraced form, which is also reflected in the unusual pattern of a row of three, or even four, front doors all together in a row. The three door pattern is usually associated with the corner of a block, often with a corner shop. The normal pattern is two doors (the left for the ground floor flat and the right for the upper flat). But in a three door pattern the extra door often led to a large L-shaped flat above the shop, (usually with an extra bedroom). Or at the end of a block the extra door might simply be to a house, often occupied by the landlord of the terrace of flats. The four door pattern is a feature of Tyneside flats built in the 1890's and reflects the simple (but very economical) device of combining the back extensions of two houses (four flats). On earlier flats, which were without the scullery extensions such an economy was not so important. However, the most important point about their terraced form is that they appeared to be terraced houses. Indeed in some areas we can detect pretensions toward middle class housing.

## The Facade

The similarity of the Tyneside flat and middle-class terraced housing becomes even clearer when we examine closely their facade. This similarity is not so apparent in the earliest Tyneside flats - nor later, cheaply built ones. They were built of poor quality brick, to minimum standards with grimly unadorned front doors and windows. The absence of a front garden, a brick wall and/or iron-railings and especially of an attic or basement accentuated the fact they were basic working-class housing. Indeed, it appears that before bye-law regulations enforced minimum standards of sanitary conditions, they were often just as insanitary as the old slums.[30] However, the later designs reveal both rising expectations of working-class housing, and many quintessentially middle-class refinements. Both reflect the general rise in the standard of living of the working class in the second half of the nineteenth century, aided by the mass production of house decorations. Typical middle class architectural features ranged from fairly major features like a small enclosed front garden, with brick and/or iron railings or bay windows or, 'false gables', designed to echo one element of rural cottages. More minor middle class features were quoinstones at the end of a terrace to give a sense of affluence, or a unifying course of stone the whole length of the terrace that gave a sense of respectability to the block. A host of decorative features also echoed middle class taste: The doorway was a focus of many key decorations. The more impressive the doorway, the more respectable the occupant. (See the illustrations at the end of this chapter for a photographic survey of these features).

Of course, Tyneside flats were not unique in assimilating middle-class decorative fashions. Stefan Muthesius claims that by 1900 a working-class terraced house usually contained more decoration than a middle-class house had done in 1800.[31] Increasingly the Tyneside flat was built to accommodate the 'labour aristocracy' of the working-class, and, even later, lower middle class families, and the absorption of these decorative features gives us an insight into the prevailing attitudes and expectations of their occupants and of their builders and landlords.

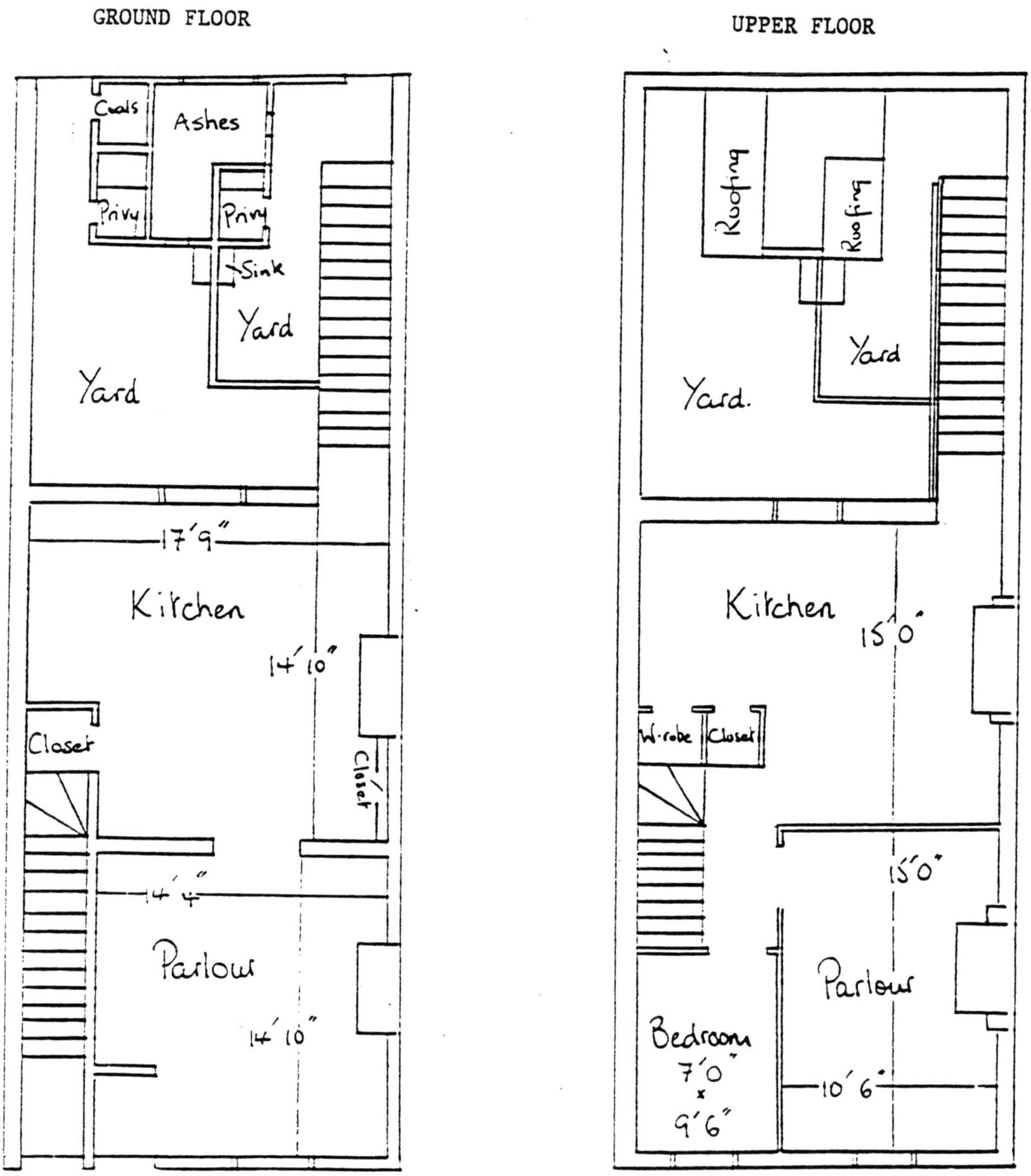


PLANS OF 2/3 ROOM TYNESIDE FLATS, BYKER HILL.
(Not to scale)

Source: Newcastle Corporation Building Plans 8th December 1868

## The Internal Layout

The typical layout of the 2/3 room Tyneside flat can be seen from the following plan.

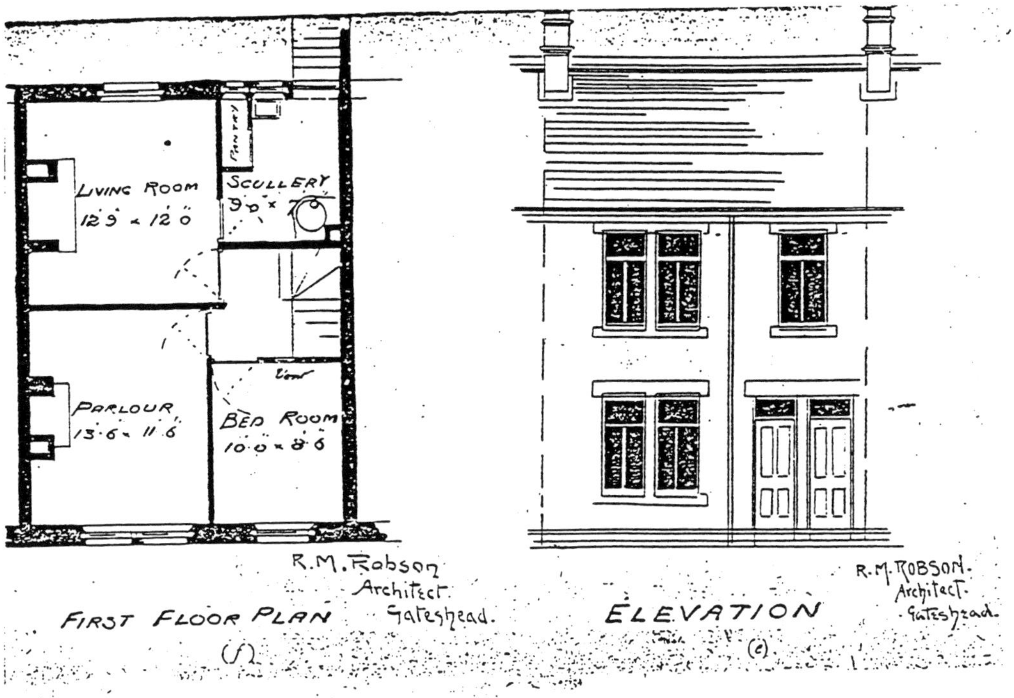


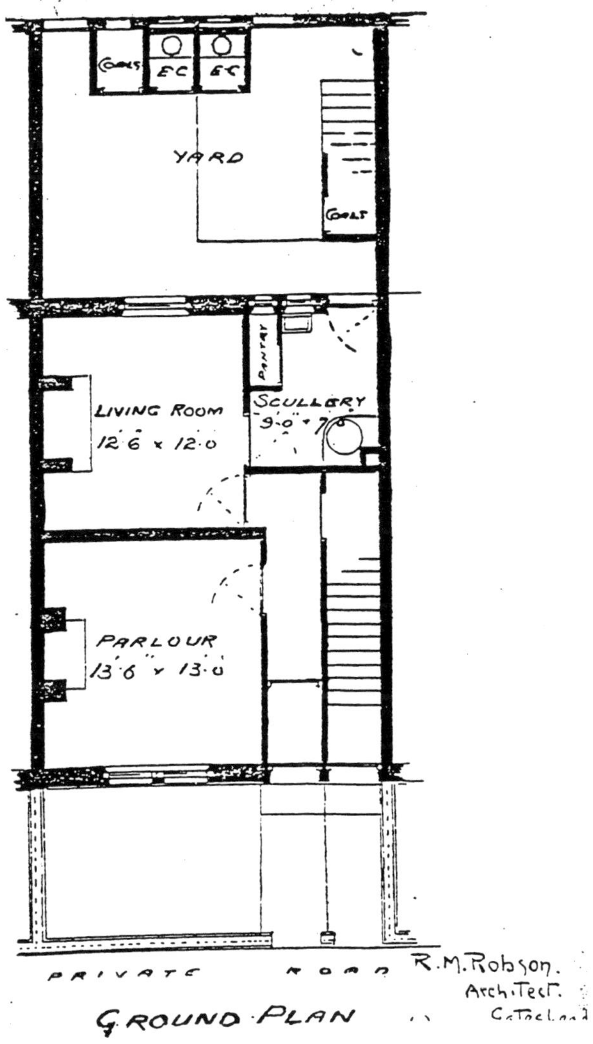


Plans of Tyneside Flat (1902)

Source: John Whitburn, (1902)
pp.45-47

The right door opens directly into the parlour of the ground floor flat and the kitchen/scullery has a back door that leads out to its backyard. The left door leads to the upper flat via a staircase, usually with a tiny landing from which the three rooms could be entered. (A tiny bedroom built above the stairs was the extra room). From the kitchen/scullery a flight of open stairs led to its separate backyard. The backyards were an important part of the design of Tyneside flats. From 1866 they were to be a minimum of one quarter of the whole building plot.[32] The backyard preserved the nature of the separate flats by ensuring privacy even at the rear, accomplished by a dividing wall, and separate back gates, toilets and coal facilities. The main difference between the earlier flats and the later ones can be seen from R M Robson's plans. They show that a scullery has been added, allowing an extra living room. The dimensions show that the rooms were still small in 1902, especially the scullery and first floor bedroom. The unusual depth of Tyneside flats is also shown by the plans created by a layout of one room wide and two deep - the reverse of a terrace house. This meant that Tyneside flats used the building plot more economically, as we shall see later. It also meant that their rooms were often very gloomy, especially at the back. Very few, very small rooms, gloomy interiors and high density developments contrast starkly with middle class terraced houses, and yet these shortcomings were efficiently masked by their frontages.

## Newcastle's Bye-Law Building Regulations

Local bye-laws were a vital means by which councils sought to tackle the nineteenth century problems associated with urbanisation. The building regulations were based on a series of public health acts, which were at first permissive and only later compulsory. The issue of public health and poor housing conditions were closely interlocked, stimulating many directives to improve sanitary conditions which naturally directly affected housing. All new houses were to be built within prescribed standards of sanitation, and boards of Public Health were created to ensure compliance. The main elements of public health were proper drainage, adequate sewers and toilets, clean water supplies and sufficient 'air-space'. Air-space was a corner-stone of bye-law building regulations, directly affecting the size and ventilation of 'habitable rooms', the width of streets, and the amount of open space around individual dwellings. The emphasis upon open-space was founded on the mistaken Victorian belief that disease was primarily airborne. Stefan Muthesius and M J Daunton emphasise the influence of local bye-laws on the development of diverse regional forms of working-class housing. They argue that the latitude to interpret - or even ignore - relevant acts of parliament (up to the 1870's) explains the diverse solutions to the housing problem reflected in many regional house-types. They both concentrate upon the Tyneside flat and Newcastle's 1866 bye-laws to demonstrate their thesis.

Muthesius argues that terraced housing for the working-classes was the product of "northern planning ingenuity" formulated within local bye-law regulations.[33] Economical land-use and the ubiquitous backyard are highlighted as their most basic elements, the latter being enclosed and private and thereby "the essential new element" in urban housing. Daunton emphasises this transition to an enclosed, private house-style and settlement pattern of the working-classes. He describes the older traditional forms as "promiscuous" in the private domain and "cellular" in the public domain. These technical terms are meant to convey the traditional sharing of space and facilities in a communal way. By contrast the new forms are described as "encapsulated" and "open", meaning that the private domain became enclosed and private (no longer shared water and toilet facilities, for instance), and the public domain more open (unlike courts and alleys), causing public space to be more regulated and accessible. The significance of this transition will be considered later.

Tyneside flats are a variant of terraced housing according to Muthesius, and since he notices the effect of bye-laws on the latter he concludes that bye-laws were a formative influence on many of the features of Tyneside flats. The height of their ceilings (nine feet), the width of their front and back streets (forty and twenty feet respectively) and the amount of open space (backyards) are all stipulated by Newcatle's 1866 bye-laws. However, he gives no interpretation of the significance of bye-laws on the subsequent prevalence of Tyneside flats. He merely notes that they were an indigenous house-type, a variant of terraced housing, which easily adapted to bye-law regulations.

M J Daunton goes much further: he describes bye-law housing as a "discrete phase" in the history of working-class housing. He writes:

> "when the constriction of the built-up area was removed in the 1860's, and the first building bye-laws were imposed, the new accommodation which was provided on the available land institutionalised the pragmatic solution which had emerged. The Tyneside flat resulted from the predominant form of subdivided property, adjusted to accord with the building bye-laws, and extended to the suburban land which became available in the 1860's."[34]

The ambiguity of the claim of an indigenous house-type has already been noted. But which bye-laws 'institutionalised' Tyneside flats? Both Muthesius and Daunton emphasise clause 12 of Newcatle's 1866 Bye-law building regulations. It states,

> "Every.....dwelling house, shall have, in the rear or at the side thereof, an open space, exclusively belonging thereto,....equal to an

area to at least one fourth of...the entire area of the ground occupied."[35]

Daunton writes of the clause,

> "[It] was a standard attempt to prevent a promiscuous sharing of space in the future, and a similar provision was contained in the bye-laws of other towns. But it was only on Tyneside that the terraced-flat developed. <u>The bye-laws prevented the construction of tenements</u>, but did not positively require the erection of flats. The Tyneside flat was an ingenious way of providing a backyard equal to a fourth of the property, specific to the individual unit."[36]

But he does not explain why other towns with similar regulations did not develop Tyneside flats. No does he explain <u>how</u> this clause discriminated against tenements. Are we meant to conclude it was too uneconomical to devote a quarter of the land to open space? But no evidence of this is given. Lastly, he implies a deliberate policy to discourage tenements, which conversely suggests a policy to encourage Tyneside flats (despite his disclaimer).

Therefore it is surprising to discover that Newcastle's Report of Public Health in 1866 shows that in twenty other towns a minimum of one third of property for open space was not unusual.[37] Indeed, the first draft of clause 12 stipulated a minimum of a third of new property be open space. Nevertheless Daunton is correct to suppose that the bye-laws were one factor that discouraged tenements - but he overlooks another regulation; for clause 2 stages:

> "No building hereafter to be erected, in any street hereafter to be made, shall at any time be built of, or raised to, a greater number of storeys than the houses for which such street has been made."[38]

This would effectively exclude tenements from the new residential suburbs, unless they were built in isolated positions, which would be impractical because that would entail primary drainage and sewerage systems and new roads. The only alternative sites would be in central Newcastle where buildings of four or more storeys was the norm. But here the land-values were prohibitive for new tenements. And bye-laws that stipulated deeper walls for higher builders would act as another discouragement towards tenements.[39]

However, the debate about the Report of Public Health in 1866 reveals another discouragement to tenements. Mr Gregson remarked that the lack of tenements in Newcastle

> "had been caused by an act of [the] Council .. that compel[led] landlords of tenemented property to compound for the rates. The consequence... had been that the owners of the property were compelled to pay a whole year's poor rates and borough rates, no matter how short the tenancy of the occupants might be, and this had rendered that kind of property so unprofitable that builders would not invest in it."[40]

It appears that he was referring to an act passed on 13 April 1853, long before comprehensive building regulations were formulated. It was passed by 32 votes to 3, and four of the self-confessed owners of tenements voted for it.[41]

However, the foregoing merely explains why tenements did not become the prevalent house-type in Newcastle not why Tyneside flats became prevalent, since the bye-laws clearly did not positively require the erection of flats, as Daunton admits. To do so we must examine economic and social factors.

The bye-laws did not determine the form of Tyneside flats, nor guarantee their dominance. They merely sanctioned a house-type at a crucial moment in the local economy when large numbers of houses were needed and when wages could afford better housing. Furthermore, the innate qualities of the Tyneside flat, their simplicity, versatility and cheapness made then an ideal solution at that time.

Economic & Cultural Factors

Daunton gives the most comprehensive analysis of economic factors to date, but dismisses cultural factors. He argues that the peculiar variety of English house-types can be explained by varying levels of supply and demand within the housing market. In particular he emphasises the differential between wages and rent, which he argues provides "the nearest approximation to an explanation of variations of house size and conditions."[42] However, he justly concludes that factors of supply and demand only determine house size, not house-types. To his foregoing argument he adds the influence of local bye-law regulations and physical restraints on expansion to explain the variety of house-types. The dubious nature of such theories has already been considered, but it is worth digressing simply to note that of the six house-types Daunton examines, the least typical, the Tyneside flat, is given as the example which illustrates his theories.

Land values are widely held to be the main economic factor that determines house-type. Three factors may create high land prices: physical restraints on expansion, certain forms of tenure and monopolistic land ownership. Before we consider these factors it is necessary to establish how expensive land was in Newcastle. The Royal Commission on the Housing of the Working Classes (1884-5) establishes that up to 1885 local land values were rising. One witness declared, "There is no difficulty getting land, but it is the price of land which is the difficulty."[43] Newcastle's Medical Officer of Health stated that building land cost above

£40 per yard in the city centre, above £15 to £20 per yard in the middle of the city, and about 7/6d to 9/- per yard in the suburb of Byker.[44] But this cannot tell us the cost in comparison to elsewhere. However, the commissioners clearly believed that land was expensive in Newcastle; "Has land value in your opinion anything to do with high rent? - I think so."[45] Nevertheless, we need to realise that the land referred to was mainly that within central Newcastle, where rents and land values were highest and housing conditions the worst. Tyneside flats were built mainly in the suburbs, which was where land values were lower, thus subverting the theory that high land values caused this peculiar house-type. Moreover, Muthesius cautions us to remember that the price of land was on average only 10 to 20% of the total cost of house building.[46] Furthermore, physical restraints on expansion have already been shown to be mainly confined to an historical role, in the early stages of urbanisation, and even then, to the old town rather than the suburbs. Therefore, high prices created by restraints on expansion becomes largely irrelevant for suburban expansion.

Could Newcastle's prevalent form of land tenure explain the dominance of Tyneside flats instead? M J Mortimore argues that leasehold tenure was more profitable for landowners than freehold. His assumption is based on the belief that reversion at the end of a lease allowed redevelopment or a more costly new lease. Conversely freehold tenure, he claims, lacked flexibility, causing higher prices for the sale of land. This in turn ensured that landlords and builders must maximise their investment, for instance, by building cheap, high density housing for the lower end of the market.[47]

Most of Newcastle was built on freehold land, as the Royal Commission quickly established.[48] And the link between freehold tenure and high density housing appears to be established by comparing the plot-loading ratio of four house-types shown in Figure E below. It shows that this was highest in Tyneside flats and Leeds back-to-backs - both built on freehold land.

Figure E

Density of Development in various house forms

| | Size of plot | Area of habitable rooms | Ratio of plot: rooms |
|---|---|---|---|
| | sq.ft | sq.ft | |
| Tyneside flat (Cato St. Gateshead) | 1,064 | 1,059 | 1.0 |
| Back-to-back (Hawes St. Leeds) | 768 | 700 | 0.9 |
| Through house (Arran St. Cardiff) | 1,200 | 590 | 0.5 |
| One storey cottage (Cairo St. Sunderland) | 1.275 | 449 | 0.4 |

49

But this theory is convincingly destroyed by two counter-arguments offered by Daunton. He shows that freehold developments were not always inflexible, and therefore proportionately more expensive than leasehold. In Gateshead's Northbourne estate (in which Tyneside flats were built) arrangements were made with agents and speculators that enabled individual plots of a development to be paid on completion of each house. By delaying payment it encouraged small scale speculation and gave the landowner power to regulate the type of development, and enabled him to protect the value of his remaining land by regulating the timing and speed of developments.[50]

A similar pattern of development prevailed in Newcastle too. The Royal Commissioners were told that housing in the suburbs was being built "principally by speculative builders."[51] Richard Grainger is the most famous example of a local building speculator. He is renowned for the redevelopment of central Newcastle in 1835, but it is less widely known that he bought 544 acres of the Elswick estate for a new town development. Although this was never accomplished the estate was astutely sold off piecemeal by his friend John Clayton to solve Grainger's bankruptcy.[52] Similarly small scale developments were built in Jesmond between 1877-79 by W Temple, G Douglas and J Richardson. And in Byker the Hardy and Walker Brothers did the same between 1876-78.[53]

Secondly Daunton shows that there is no obvious link between freehold tenure and small, high density housing-types. Gateshead, Newcastle, Leicester and Northampton were all built on freehold site, yet the first pair were the most densely populated towns in 1911 and the second pair the least densely populated. Similarly the link is denied by Jarrow, in which 44% of its housing was Tyneside flats even though they were built on leasehold land. Furthermore, both Stockton and Middlesborough grew spectacularly on freehold land and yet they contain no Tyneside flats.[54]

Could the structure of Newcastle's land market explain the prevalence of Tyneside flats instead? Is there evidence of large monopolistic landowners controlling the market, creating false scarcity by manipulating demand? The Royal Commissioners were told that there were "some very large, or large, at any rate" freehold landlords in Newcastle.[55] However, the general pattern appears to have been of small scale landownership and landlords. In the first half of the nineteenth century local aristocratic families like the Ridley-White's and the Blackett-Ord's had owned large estates adjoining Newcastle (in Heaton and Byker, and South Benwell, respectively). But these had been fragmented by sales to industrialists like William Armstrong or speculators like Richard Grainger and although Armstrong and Grainger amassed large estates (in Heaton and Byker, and Elswick respectively), their sales of lands fragmented landownership even more. But this does not mean there were no large landowners, only that the general pattern was not of monopolistic landowners.

Even if it had been Daunton shows that such patterns did not cause inevitably high land prices and rents. The rent index at Bradford and Cardiff was identical yet in the former under 25% of the land was owned by its three largest landowners, and in the latter over 50% was owned by its three largest landowners. Similarly Cardiff and Ipswich had an identical pattern of landownship yet the rent index of the former was 59 and of the latter was only 44.[56]

But there is a suggestion of the manipulation of the land and housing market in Newcastle, despite the absence of a general pattern of large scale landownership. The Royal Commission was alerted to an incident that occurred in the early 1870's. The Vicar of St. Johns, Newcastle, told them that the corporation had demolished slums in New Pandon in accord with new powers to demolish and rebuild better housing for slum dwellers. But no new houses had been built because a petition from landlords in Byker persuaded the corporation not to do so in competition with them when so many of their houses were unoccupied.[57] H E Armstrong, Newcastle Medical Officer, was closely questioned on the subject and his answers reveal that statutory powers designed to improve housing conditions were being used for commercial redevelopment. Only after repeated questioning would he admit that "The corporation has not in any instance rebuilt where it has pulled down."[58]

However, we need to remember again that these were policies affecting the value of land in the city centre, not the suburbs, although they did affect the demand for housing in the suburbs. Indeed, Armstrong stated that the former occupants of New Pandon went to Byker. But there is no evidence of complicity between the corporation and these landlords. In reply to a question which implied that there might be, Armstrong insisted that the empty houses in Byker were built between six and ten years before the demolition at New Pandon.[59]

The transcripts of the Royal Commission and of the proceedings of the corporation reveal two basic features of Newcastle's 'housing policy'. First, it is clear that the corporation was particularly slow in applying housing legislation to solve its housing problems. Secondly, and arising from their attitude to interventionist measures, they had an almost limitless faith in private enterprise. They felt sure that the only practicable solutions to Newcastle's housing problem lay with self-help and private enterprise. Therefore, the structure of the land market in Newcastle does not reveal large monopolistic landowners and manipulating demand in their favour, but within the land market there was scope for manipulation by local landlords, who had extra influence in the housing market because of the sympathetic attitude of the corporation towards private enterprise. The case of New Pandon is best summed up by question 7887 of the Royal Commission: "So they were afraid of competition in rents? - That is what it came to."

This brings us to the theory that the differential between wages and rent is the best explanation of the variations of house-type in England. It proposes that the lower the ratio between the two, the smaller and higher-density will be the corresponding house-type. Figure F shows the wage and rent index for 18 English provincial cities, plus London, in 1905. London's rent and wage levels are take as 100. The rent index reveals that rent levels varied far more than wage levels. The table also shows marked variation in the differential between wages and rent. Furthermore, it clearly illustrates that the smallest, highest-density house-types correspond to the lowest differentials between wages and rent. Newcastle's rent is higher than all the other provincial cities except Plymouth and Devonport. This is confirmed by the Royal Commission, which was surprised to discover than in 1885 Newcastle's rent could even be higher than London's.[60] On average the rent for Tyneside flats was about 5/6d to 6/6d, but they could be rented as low as 3/- to 3/6d at Byker.

FIGURE F

<u>Wages and rent levels in English cities, 1905</u>

| | Rent index (Skilled builders) | Wage Index | Ratio of wages to rent |
|---|---|---|---|
| London | 100 | 100 | 1.0 |
| | Subdivided property | | |
| Plymouth and Devonport | 81 | 80 | 1.0 |
| | Tyneside flats | | |
| Newcastle | 76 | 90 | 1.2 |
| Gateshead | 66 | 90 | 1.4 |
| South Shields | 61 | 88 | 1.4 |
| | Single-storey cottages | | |
| Sunderland | 59 | 88 | 1.5 |
| | Back-to-backs | | |
| Bradford | 59 | 83 | 1.4 |
| Halifax | 55 | 82 | 1.5 |
| Leeds | 56 | 87 | 1.6 |
| | Lancashire: through houses without back additions | | |
| Oldham | 60 | 92 | 1.5 |
| Burnley | 53 | 85 | 1.6 |
| Bolton | 53 | 90 | 1.7 |
| Blackburn | 50 | 87 | 1.7 |
| | Midlands and South: through houses with back additions | | |
| Cardiff | 59 | 92 | 1.6 |
| Nottingham | 56 | 92 | 1.6 |
| Birmingham | 59 | 98 | 1.7 |
| Bristol | 53 | 93 | 1.8 |
| Ipswich | 44 | 86 | 2.0 |
| Leicester | 48 | 94 | 2.0 |

Source: <u>p.p</u>.1908 CBIII, <u>Report of an enquiry by the Board of Trade into Working Class Rents, Housing and Retail Prices</u>, Table E.

However, when compared to the New Industrial Tenements, at Garth Heads (the cheapest rooms began at 2/6d to 3/3d) or city tenements (at 4/- to 4/6d) or single cellar kitchens in Newcastle (at 3/- to 5/-) it is clear that they were generally more expensive.[61] Furthermore, H E

Armstrong revealed that they were usually paid quarterly, and Rev. Houldey revealed that they were generally "let by the year".[62] The significance of this upon the social class of the occupants will be considered later.

The Royal Commission calculated that workmen earning 30/- or more per week would be the occupants of the Tyneside flats. They were told that Newcastle's artisans, especially those at Stephenson and Hawthorn's could be expected to earn in excess of 30/- per week.[63] I have been unable to investigate how well paid was Newcastle's working population, however, it is clear that in the last quarter of the nineteenth century local wages were generally rising. So too were rent levels. This period was also a very buoyant period for the local building trade. But it is important to note the sharp slump following 1875, no doubt illustrating the adverse "trade circumstances" referred to by Armstrong as the reason for so many empty houses in Byker in the 1870's.[64]

Even if we concede Daunton's claim that "The small house size and frequency of overcrowding on Tyneside is indeed explicable in terms of economics rather than convention"[65], we are still left with his admission that "economics... cannot account for the architectural response to economic restraints."[66] In other words, economics are not a sufficient explanation of the variations of house-type - only of house size.

Therefore Daunton emphasises bye-law regulations and physical restraints on expansion. However, we have already noted the flaws in his argument about Newcastle's bye-laws, and have agreed with his admission that they did not positively require Tyneside flats to be built - even though they did prevent new tenements. We also noted earlier that the physical restraints on expansion are overemphasised, indeed, virtually irrelevant to the prevalence of Tyneside flats in Newcastle's suburbs. He also implies that Tyneside flats are the best house-type to explain the peculiar variations of English housing, yet they are the most unrepresentative form - only 2.9% of England's housing in 1911! And he relies on Newcastle's experience to support his research into Gateshead's Tyneside flats!

Crucially Daunton dismissively omits a key factor: In his opinion cultural factors are merely "a desperate refuge" for those unable to construct a convincing economic explanation of the variations in English house-types.[67] But it need not be viewed in this way. Even though cultural factors are notoriously difficult to describe and quantify, they complement an economic analysis and can permit a comprehensive and sophisticated explanation of the prevalence of Newcastle's Tyneside flats.

H A Mess' conclusion that explanations "of a purely economic nature are not by themselves... adequate", is surely correct, and he is on the right track when he refers to an established Tyneside "custom and... habit of mind...[in which] the small and congested home is accepted as a matter of course... to a degree greater than elsewhere."[68] Daunton is right to discard Mess's theory about Tyneside's "historical backwardness", which underpins his tentative cultural explanation. It makes Tynesiders appear like some sort of primitive tribe shielded from 'civilisation' by their geographical and historical isolation. But he is wrong to dismiss cultural factors altogether.

It is necessary to view these cultural factors from two perspectives. Firstly that of the dominant ruling classes - Newcastle's corporation, and those with real influence upon its policies. And secondly that of the working classes themselves. But before doing so it is germane to incorporate Sutcliffe's theory about the far-reaching effect of "the urban variable" on modern English history. In a complex argument he claims that the varied response of English towns to government legislation designed to solve the housing problem led to the present imposition of centralised uniform regulations and directives.[69] The considerable latitude permitted by permissive legislation was remarked upon earlier, and explains diverse bye-law building regulations, which was an ambivalent influence upon regional house-types. But as Sutcliffe's perspective is the spatial development and physical environment of towns it allows us to view Tyneside flats as a product of this urban variable. A crucial component of the urban variable was the creation of what has been called 'urbanism' - a distinct urban culture. This arose, he claims, from consumption patterns in the cities which caused "a complex of processes which create and maintain the physical environment."[70] In particular he means the growing "neighbourhood orientated" working classes, with an immobile surplus labour force - the residuum - "which produced a growing segregation into culturally homogeneous areas".[71] Therefore it also enables us to see the Tyneside flat - and all forms of housing - as the concrete expression of prevalent cultural values.

By nature Newcastle's corporation was politically very conservative. As early as 1853 the report of the Sanitary committee urged "An example ought to be set by the Corporation and by individuals, in constructing Houses for the Habitation of the humbler classes..."[72] In 1866 Mr Lowthian Bell, argued that it was "within the powers, scope and duty" of the council to initiate new housing.[73] Yet in 1876 Mr J P Robinson complained that despite accepting Mr Bell's resolution (in diluted form) "nothing had been done, except the houses in the New Road."[74] Middlebrook notes that they were very slow to use the powers granted to them by successive housing acts and remarks that "It was not until well into the first decade of the new century that the corporation at last made a determined effort to tackle the housing problem."[75]

Indeed the corporation always preferred to look to private enterprise to provide the necessary housing. Even the new tenements built in New Road, (Garth Heads) were built by private enterprise.[76] But why did the corporation so adamantly resist intervening directly? Undoubtedly Newcastle was not unique; many other towns resisted such measures for just as long. It was partly due to the national ethos of laissez-faire and self-help entrepreneuship. But it is vital to remember that many members of the council were landowners or landlords, as the Royal Commission discovered.[77] Furthermore, other members were prominent businessmen, professionals and industrialists. This is not to imply that such members abused their authority - although this is likely in some cases.

However, for decades Newcastle was the example of private enterprise and entrepreneurship - embodied by contemporary heroes like George and Robert Stephenson and William Armstrong, and many others. Therefore, it is unsurprising that the corporation had an almost inexhaustible faith in such values. Moreover, the council debate about public health in 1866 shows that they were keen to keep down their rates. This meant vetoing or minimising initiatives and reliance upon private enterprise. Furthermore, lower rates were designed to favour private enterprise, and high rates "looked like taxing one class for the benefit of another" - undermining the fundamental principles of self-help.[78]

This introduces the subject of class. In their efforts to solve the housing problem two different attitudes are evident. Firstly, the dominant ruling class differentiated between their own values and those of their inferiors. This was manifested in many ways, including the segregation into culturally homogeneous areas referred to by Sutcliffe. Secondly they differentiated between an undeserving and a deserving working class; (or an irresponsible and a responsible working class).

In 1854 Newcastle's Temperance Society proposed that cleanliness and temperance would solve the serious public health problem. They advocated a two part solution. For the poorer classes public baths, wash houses and model lodging houses should be provided. But for the 'operative classes' improved dwellings should be built. They urged employers to follow the good example of coal-owners (in truth, not much of a recommendation).[79] Even thirty years later the distinction was still made. George Laws (Newcastle's Town Surveyor) told the Royal Commission that even two-roomed Tyneside flats were "too good for working men", but suitable for artisans.[80]

In 1872 Nicholas Gibson advocated a solution to Newcastle's housing problem which is very similar to that above. However, its difference is that it now advocates an appropriate house-style for the responsible working class. Earlier we noted his agreement with the opinion of the Duchess of Lothair; "I am much in favour of improved dwellings for the poor, but then you must take care that your *cottages are not villas*."[81] (Gibson's italics). Furthermore, he also proposed that private enterprise should build such "healthy, cheap and convenient" cottages, which he claimed could be profitable investments.

Let us pause to consider the relevance of such attitudes to the later prevalence of Tyneside flats. The dominant ruling class begin by differentiating between their own values and that of their social inferiors. Next they distinguish between the irresponsible and responsible working classes. They advocate an appropriate standard of public health facilities and housing form for each, thereby encouraging a cultural segregation between the residuum and the 'labour aristocracy'. Finally they advocate an appropriate style of house for the responsible working classes which will emulate middle class values (the cottage style) and yet distinguish them from the middle classes. Such attitudes are the ideological counterparts of the cultural segregation described by Sutcliffe, and reflected in the Tyneside flat, and working class terraced housing in general.

The last deduction is explicit in a favourable review of Bannister Fletcher's book Model Houses for the Industrial Classes in The Building News, November 1871. He was an architect/housing reformer who reacted against drab barrack style tenements. The elevation of his design was commended for disguising the fact that it contained flats and for giving "the idea that the house is the residence of some respectable member of the 'lower middle' class, and this effect", they wrote, "is further supported by a low dwarf wall in front with stone coping, surmounted by a simple iron bar and standards".[82]

The elevation bears close resemblance to Tyneside flats built in the 1880's and 90's. (Compare the elevations, in the illustrations at the end of this chapter). Furthermore, the houses and flats of Buston Terrace, Jesmond, give a clear example of the similarities between middle class terraced houses and Tyneside flats. They face each other and share very similar stone lintels over the front doors, and identical stone mounted door bells and dwarf walls. Even the bay windows are similar, except that they are confined to the ground floor on the houses.

Earlier we noted that the design of Tyneside flats represented a compromise between middle class terraced housing and working class tenements. We can now see them as a concrete expression of the cultural hegemony of the dominant middle classes. This hegemony was expressed in other ways apart from the facade of the Tyneside flat. We noted earlier that the terraced form permitted an 'encapsulated' private domain and an open, regulated public domain. In other words greater privacy was not only a means to improve sanitation but it also promoted middle class values like privacy and single family occupation. A regulated open public domain was also easier to police than 'cellular' patterns of courtyards (as we are re-learning today). We also noted earlier that it was easy to incorporate corners shops into terraces of Tyneside flats. These were also vehicles to propagate middle class values, and as many were owned by local landlords it often ensured the custom of local tenants.

This close link between house form and social control is explicit in the proposals of Newcastle's Temperance Society referred to above;

> "why not the same provision of a superior class of house in connection with each large manufacturing establishment, a model village named after the firm, having all the requirements of sanitary improvements educational, moral and recreative institutions, benefit societies, savings banks, building societies and other approved modes of investment? Good tenants would be secured, and we have little doubt but that on well-defined conditions (without risk or cost to any company) many builders would engage in such undertakings".[83]

All that has been proposed so far about cultural factors is applicable to all working class housing. Therefore, it cannot necessarily explain the peculiar prevalence of Tyneside flats in Newcastle. Other forms of terraced housing could have been built under similar circumstances. It is necessary at this juncture to consider the attitudes of the working classes, and to relate them to economic factors. Firstly, we should acknowledge that Mess is correct to mention the 'traditional' occupancy of small, overcrowded homes in Tyneside. Whilst this long history of overcrowding need not mean the acceptance of slum conditions it does establish that even slight improvements would represent real gains. Therefore it would make it more acceptable to the providers and consumers to build a small house size. The history of sub-divided slum tenements would make terraced flats acceptable, even attractive in comparison. From the builders' point of view high land values would encourage a high density house-type. Lastly, it was necessary to build a house-type which would attract the best paid working classes. Therefore, the design needed to be cheap, and within the current expectations and aspirations of its intended tenants.

However, it is incorrect to give the impression that Newcastle's working classes were content with slum conditions, which Mess implies. The 'tradition' was dictated by circumstances rather than a ready acceptance of one or two room homes, symptomatic of the 'historical backwardness' proposed by Mess. The Royal Commissioners were told that many workers stayed in the slums because they preferred to be near their work. For those already rising at 3 or 4 o'clock in the morning an additional 1 or 2 mile walk was unwelcome - especially uphill at the end of an exhausting day. Until suburban tramways became available this was a real discouragement to accept better housing in the suburbs, as were heavy fines for lateness.[84]

Nevertheless, once the income of the working classes rose - especially that of the artizan class - it was important that their housing should improve too. Part of the versatility of the design of Tyneside flats arises from their ability to incorporate improvements - extra rooms, extensions, bay-windows, generally improved facades. As we have seen this was especially important when the occupants wished to emulate middle class values.

Conclusion

The explanations of the peculiar regional house-type and of the prevalence of Newcastle's Tyneside flats defy definitive conclusions. Therefore, simplistic emphasis upon the origins of the house-type or historical and geographical influences before urbanisation are only of limited value. The influences of urbanisation - rapid surburban growth, endemic overcrowding and all the attendant problems of poor housing - are of far greater relevance.

However, the bye-law building regulations which were one response to urbanisation, were mainly permissive and passive influences upon the success of Tyneside flat. And although they eliminated tenements as an alternative house type they did not prevent terraced housing (rather than flats) being built. They did not positively require Tyneside flats to be built, merely that they conform to regulations.

The above are secondary factors, which cannot be said of economic influences. However, the interpretation of the operation of economic factors is fraught with difficulties. As a generalisation, it is fair to correlate small house size with high land prices, freehold tenure, a restrictive land and housing market, and a low wages/rent ratio. To a degree all of these factors fit Newcastle between 1850-1900. But when tested by empirical evidence these generalisations lose their validity when too strictly applied to Newcastle. More research is needed into Newcastle's land and house market, incorporating comparisons with other English provincial cities. And a far more comprehensive evaluation of Newcastle's working classes wages/rent ratio is needed, to test its validity more thoroughly and to permit more comprehensive comparisons with other regions. But economic factors only help to explain the house size of Tyneside flats - not their particular form. Unless linked to cultural factors, and thereby to historical and geographical factors, economic explanations merely become reductionist.

There is far more scope to this approach than I have been able to explore here. Much more could be done with literary sources, by drawing upon biographical, fictional and descriptive sources which are written from various social class perspectives. For instance, Jack Common's Kiddar's Luck reveals the attitudes of one section of working class occupants of Tyneside flats. Similarly the 'condition of England' novels might prove valuable sources. A wider selection of central and local government documents - including the wording of Acts of Parliament - might also be productive.

Lastly, the intrinsic merits of the design of Tyneside flats needs to be given greater emphasis in their dominance in Newcastle. It is necessary to acknowledge that the form of a house is itself an historical source, if used correctly. The fact that Tyneside flats embodied cultural values and traditions is borne out by their continued construction, the post-modernist marina development at St Peter's Basic contains examples of this enduring housing form.

KIT PEARCE

**Plate 4.**
Post 1945 Tyneside flats. Armstrong Road, Elswick.

**Plate 5.**
Tyneside flats with gabled bays. Seventh Avenue, Heaton.

**Plate 6.**
Flats, a single dwelling and retail units. Fenham Road.

**Plate 7.**
Canopies, bay windows and two and three door entrances. Farndale Road, Benwell.

**Plate 8.**
Most inexpensive of its type.
Four door entrance Tyneside flats. Pearson Street, Walker.

**Plate 9.**
Middle class terraced villas?
Doorways to Tyneside flats.
Hampstead Road, Benwell.

**Plate 10.**
Rear stairways giving the upper flat access to the back yard.
Strathmore Crescent, Benwell.

## NOTES

1. <u>Census of England and Wales, 1911</u>. Volume VI, Buildings of Various Kinds, Tables 1 and 2

2. M J Daunton, <u>House and Home in the Victorian City, Working Class House 1850-1914</u>, (London, 1983), p.39

3. Anthony Sutcliffe, (ed) <u>Multi-Storey Living; The British Working-Class Experience</u>, (London, 1974), <u>Introduction</u>: p.8

4. Sutcliffe, p.7

5. Sutcliffe, pp.14-15

6. Stefan Muthesius, <u>The English Terraced House</u>, (Yale, 1982), p.130

7. Muthesius, p.130
(a) separate rear facilities, (b) corridors allowing separate access to each room, (c) unusually high ceilings (nine feet high), and (d) the unusual width of the house

8. Muthesius, p.101

9. J N Tarn, <u>Working-Class Housing in Nineteenth Century Britain,</u> (London, 1971), p.6

10. Daunton, p.21

11. Burnett J (1986), <u>A Social History of Housing 1815-1985</u>, Second Edition, (London), p.7

12. Mingay G E (1986), <u>The Transformation of Britain 1830-1939, The Making of Britain,</u> Volume 5, (London), p.5

13. Fraser C M and Emsley K (1973), <u>Tyneside, City and Country Histories,</u> (Newton Abbot), p.119

14. Middlesbrook S (1950), <u>Newcastle upon Tyne: Its Growth and Achievement</u>, (Newcastle), p.243

15. Fraser and Emsley, p.121

16. Benwell Community Development Project (1973), <u>Private Housing and the Working Class</u>, (Newcastle), p.21

17. Newcastle Architecture Workshop (1979), <u>Housing in Byker</u>, (Newcastle), p.60

18. Middlebrook, p.195

19. pp. 1854 XXXV, Report of the Commissioners appointed to inquire into the causes which have led to or have aggravated the late outbreak of cholera in the towns of Newcastle upon Tyne, Gateshead and Tynemouth, p.viii

20. Mess H A (1928) Industrial Tyneside (Newcastle), pp.85-88

21. Proceedings of the Newcastle Council (1867), Volume 20, March p.252

22. Proceedings, pp.242-268, (Mr Gregson)

23. Tarn J N (1971), Working-Class Housing in Nineteenth Century Britain, (London), p.6

24. Burnett J p.136 They cost £1,950 each to build and gave only 1½% return on their capital

25. Gibson N (1872), Sandringham: Its Lessons An open letter written to the mayor of Newcastle upon Tyne, 31 January 1872, p.18

26. The Newcastle Temperance Society (1854), Newcastle As It Is, Reviewed in its Moral Aspects, Social State and Sanitary Condition, (Newcastle), pp.65-6

27. Building Plans, 25 February 1862, of 3 houses, two in flats, at Essex Street, Elswick

28. Build Plans, 23 November 1876, a row of 16 houses in flats, Norfolk Road, Byker

29. Building Plans, 19 May 1881, a row of 6 houses, in flats, at the corner of Albion Road and Byker Bank

30. Newcastle upon Tyne Corporation, The Report of the Sanitary Committee, 12 October 1853, pp.166-7 "Some modern streets and lanes have been formed by speculations in those townships which were added to the Borough under the Municipal Reform Act which are scarcely less calculated to generate disease than the closely packed habitations of Sandgate".

31. Muthesius, p.242

32. Gibson J F (1881), Newcastle upon Tyne Improvement Acts and Bye-Laws 1837-1877 (Newcastle), 1866 Bye-Laws, Clause 12, p.268

33. Muthesius, p.135

34. Daunton, p.87

35. Gibson J F (ed) (1881) Newcastle upon Tyne Improvement Acts and Bye-Laws, 1837-1877, (Newcastle), p.268

36. Daunton, p.21

37. Report of Public Health in 1866, p.100

38. Gibson, p.265

39. Gibson, pp.266-7

40. Proceedings of the Newcastle Council 20 March 1867, p.259

41. Proceedings, 13 April 1853, pp.57-59

42. Daunton, p.82

43. Royal Commission on the Housing of the Working Classes 1884-85, Volume II, Q7367 and Q7418

44. Royal Commission, Q7614

45. Royal Commission, Q7613 The previous question states "witnesses have given us figures which in many cases compare unfavourably even with London..."

46. Muthesius, p.140

47. Mortimore M J (1963), Urban Growth in Bradford and Environs 1800-1960, (M A Leeds, 1963), p.p.134-5, and Landownership and Urban Growth in Bradford and its environs in the West Riding Conurbation 1850-1950, Transactions of the Institute of British Geographers, 46 (1969), pp.105-18
In Daunton pp.65-68

48. Royal Commission, Q7417

49. Daunton, p 65

50. Daunton, pp.65-68

51. Royal Commission, Q7383

52. Benwell Community Development Project, 1973 Private Housing and the Working-Class, (Newcastle) p.26

53. Barke M and Buswell R J (eds) 1980 Historical Atlas of Newcastle upon Tyne, (Newcastle Polytechnic) p.35 Types of Housing Development, C C Taylor

54. Daunton, p.65

55. Royal Commission, Q7632

56. Daunton, p.77

57. Royal Commission, Q7483, Q7620, Q7696 and Q8411

58. Royal Commission, Q7821

59. Royal Commission, Q7885

60. Royal Commission, Q7490, Q7494, Q7734 and Q8426

61. Royal Commission, Q7358, Q7392 and Q7481

62. Royal Commission, Q7734, Q7490

63. Royal Commission, Q7495

64. Royal Commission, Q7696

65. Daunton, p.81

66. Daunton, p.84

67. Daunton, p.61

68. Mess H A p.87

69. Sutcliffe A _In Search of the Urban Variable in_ Fraser D and Sutcliffe A (eds), p.83 _The Pursuit of Urban History_, (London), pp.234-263

70. Sutcliffe, p.243

71. Sutcliffe, p.244-5

72. Proceedings of Newcastle Council, 12 October 1853

73. Proceedings of Newcastle Council, 20 March 1866, p.252

74. Proceedings of Newcastle Council, 6 September 1876, p.371

75. Middlebrook, p.284, The first council houses were built in 1909 at St Lawrence, Walker and included Tyneside flats.

76. The tenements at Garth Heads were built in 1876 by the New Industrial Dwellings Company

77. Royal Commission, Q7670-1

78. Proceedings, 20 March 1867, Mr Hammond, p.259

79. Newcastle As It Is, 1854

80 Royal Commission, Q8425

81. N Gibson, p.18

82. The Building News, Vol.21, November 1871, p.319

83. Newcastle As It is, pp.65-6

84. Royal Commission, Q7498-9, Q8438

Bibliography

A. Primary Sources

1. Parliamentary Papers

Report ... to inquire into the causes ... of cholera P.P. 1854, XXXV.

Royal Commission on the Housing of the Working Classes, P.P. 1884-5, XXX, Vol.2.

Census of England and Wales, 1911, Volume VI.

2. Newcastle upon Tyne Corporate - Official Papers

Building Plans, 1850-1964.

Bye-Law Building Regulations
[in J F Gibson, Newcastle upon Tyne Improvement Acts and Bye Laws, 1837-1877, (Newcastle, 1881)]

Proceedings of the Newcastle Council
(13 April 1853, pp.56-69; 5 December 1866, pp.50, 51;
20 March 1867, pp.242-269).

Report of the Sanitary Committee, 1853

Report of Public Health in 1853

3. The Housing Debate

The Building News, Vol.21, Nov.3 1871; pp.319-21.

Gibson N, 1872, Sandringham : Its Lessons : An open letter written to the Mayor of Newcastle upon Tyne.

Newcastle Temperance Society 1854 : Newcastle As It Is : Reviewed in its Moral Aspects, Social State and Sanitary Condition.

Walsham Sir John, Three Reports on the state of Dwellings of the Labouring Classes in Northumberland, Cumberland, Durham and Westmoreland, (Newcastle, 1840).

Whitburn John, 1902, The Housing Problem in Newcastle upon Tyne, Newcastle.

B. Secondary Sources

1. Main Sources
Daunton M J, 1983, House and Home in the Victorian City Working-Class Housing 1850-1914

Muthesius S, 1982, The English Terraced House, Yale

Sutcliffe A (ed) 1974, Multi-Storey Living: The British Working-Class Experience, London

Ibid, 1983, In Search of the Urban Variable, Britain in the Later Nineteenth Century, in Derek Fraser and Anthony Sutcliffe (eds), The Pursuit of Urban History, London

2. General Histories of Housing

Burnett J, 1986, A Social History of House 1815-1985, Second Edition, London

Gauldie E, 1974, Cruel Habitations, London

Mingay G E, 1986, The Transformation of Britain 1830-1939, The Making of Britain, Vol. 5 (London, 1986)

Tarn J N  Working-Class Housing in Nineteenth Century Britain, London

3. Histories of Newcastle upon Tyne and Tyneside

Barke M and Buswell R J (eds) 1980, Historical Atlas of Newcastle upon Tyne, Newcastle Polytechnic

Benwell Community Development Project 1973, Private Housing and the Working Class, Newcastle

Fraser C M and Emsley K 1973, Tyneside, City and County Histories, Newton Abbot

Mess H A 1928, Industrial Tyneside, London

Middlebrook S, 1950, Newcastle upon Tyne : Its Growth and Achievement, Newcastle

## WORKING CLASS OWNER OCCUPATION AND SOCIAL DIFFERENTIATION ON INTER-WAR TYNESIDE

### Introduction

This study is concerned with the impact of a new tenure form - mass owner occupation - on the social structure of Tyneside between the wars. There had been a significant element of owner-occupation before the first world war but it was not distinctive in form or location from the housing stock provided by private landlords for renting, the major element in the housing system which comprised some 90% of all accommodation. The real growth in mass owner-occupation was not to occur until the 1960s and subsequently. However the 20s and 30s are of very great importance because in this period the largely new system of private building for owner occupiers who financed the purchase of their dwellings by mortgages was put together in its modern form. This included the development of existing relations among builders, 'exchange professionals'(solicitors, estate agents and accountants), and finance capital from a concern with the organization of the provision of privately rented accommodation towards the modern system which underpins mass owner occupation. This change in direction of the 'urban bourgeoisie' resulted from the impact of working class organization on the existing tenure system during the first world war (see Melling 1980, Damer 1980) and had to develop in conflict with a very serious competitor in the form of council housing.

Things were not settled in the 1930s. Indeed after the second world war it looked for a time as if good quality council housing was going to triumph as the mass ordinary housing tenure in the United Kingdom in general and in Scotland and the North of England in particular. It would be foolish to assert that the reasons why this did not happen were 'determined'' by events in the 1920s and 30s, but the underlying tensions which caused things to develop as they did were very evident in the earlier period, and an examination of it is helpful in understanding subsequent events.

As is so often the case with any discussion of the social history of Tyneside, inter-war housing developments cannot be understood without a recognition of the extra-ordinary prosperity of the conurbation before 1919 and an understanding of the continuation of elements of that prosperity right through the slump. Tyneside's prosperity pre and during the Great War was based on high wages in manufacturing industry, especially heavy engineering and shipbuilding, and in mining. The high wages reflected a high level of demand for skilled and/or physically very fit labour. This demand resulted in massive in migration. This in migration was the major cause of the housing problem. Thus in the debate around the 1908 Housing and Town Planning Bill (Hansard 12th May 1908) the major locations of overcrowding in mainland Britain were identified as Clydebank, Coventry and Gateshead, in each case in consequence of industrial development and the inability of housing delivery systems to keep pace with population growth. The way in which this housing crisis was taken up by the local labour movement has been described in Byrne 1980, 1982, North Tyneside CDP 1977-2 - and Benwell CDP 1979. It is very important to remember that population growth continued throughout the 1914-18 war in a period when almost no housing was built.

The form and impact of war time agitation about rent levels has been described extensively (Melling 1980, Damer 1980, Beirne 1977) and the way in which popular concern about housing conditions was interpreted as a threat to public order and system stability has likewise been documented(Swennarton 1981, Gilbert 1970).The implementation of the Addison, Chamberlain and Wheatley housing acts (i.e. the two acts of 1919 and the acts of 1923 and 24) laid the foundations of good quality council housing and a state supported system of owner occupation. However if we are to understand what happened we have to recognize that developments in the 1920s had no direct relationship with the problem of the slums. What emerged were two competing tenures for the aristocracy of labour, both subsidized by the state and both dependent on state organization. Although that dependency was far greater for council housing, it was by no means absent in the private sector where local authorities provided land, mortgages and mortgage guarantees in addition to cash subsidies for that part of private sector development which was within the reach of whitecollar and highly paid manual workers. We also have to understand that the future of the two tenures was fought out in the politics of the local state(see Byrne 1980) where the urban bourgeoisie were strongly represented as non-socialist elected representatives. Indeed from this period onwards the urban bourgeoisie was to provide almost the only representative basis for capital as industrial capitalists had very largely withdrawn from Tyneside local government.

Tyneside had four related housing problems in 1919.The first was an absolute shortage of housing accommodation in the wake of a war when there was a great deal of new household formation. The second was the difference in standards between pre 1914 and post 1919 construction. This was very much a matter of comparative amenity. The older housing, as opposed to Tyneside flats, was often larger in floor area and both houses and Tyneside flats were substantially better built. Typically building regulations were relaxed post 1919 to allow for far lower ceiling heights and new construction techniques which produced less solid dwellings. However the new construction was all built with modern amenities ie. hot water, baths, inside WCs and electricity. It was also usually built in pleasant layouts with gardens in contrast to the grid iron high density streets of Tyneside terraces. This layout was of course a function of cheaper land values consequent on new transport technologies, especially motor buses. The third problem was that of overcrowding. Tyneside flats built after the 1860s were certainly not slums in terms of either physical or social characteristics. However, they were not always large and household densities could be very high. Finally there was the problem of the slums, typically pre 1860s housing often built for the middle and upper classes (eg.Barnes Close in Gateshead - see Byrne et al, 1985) but now let off as tenements in the English sense i.e. as one room dwellings with shared amenities. These dwellings were always absolutely defective in sanitary terms and were usually overcrowded.

When considering the origins of mass owner occupation the conditions of the slums are largely irrelevant. Slum dwellers did not become owner occupiers in the inter war period nor indeed subsequently. However the skilled working class family with relatively high wages, especially wages which were multiple, (and they were quite likely to be in families living in flats but overcrowded), could substantially better their housing conditions by moving into either this tenure or 1920s council housing. Although some pre 1914 flats and terraced houses were improved by the addition of amenities in the inter war years, state subsidies did not go beyond the replacement of earth by water closets (although this was massive in scale, especially in Gateshead - see Manders 1974). In fact the 'modernization' of pre 1914 housing was largely done in the 1970s. If a family of five wanted separate bedrooms for parents and the children of each sex (shared) together with a bath and hot water, then they were likely to have to move to post 1919 housing because the pre 1914 stock which had such amenities was very expensive. This issue of access to amenities is very important. Karn and Ungerson sensibly point out the importance of this neglected factor in tenure choice (1980) and the massive significance of hot water for women is evident to anyone with memories of living in a dwelling without a hot water supply, a common enough experience for any Tynesider brought up in the 40s or 50s as was the present author. It should be noted that almost all pre 1914 Tyneside flats and much terraced housing,including much which survives as good quality stock to this day, was not built with bathrooms and WCs and would rely on a difficult and dirty backboiler for water heating if it had a hot water supply at all.

Implicit in this discussion so far has been the notion that the significant social division on Tyneside lay in the interwar years, as indeed it still does, not between manual and whitecollar workers but between well paid and poorly paid manual workers. The skilled manual working class and 'white collar' workers had far more in common than the skilled manual had with the poor. This was not just a matter of income, although there was a considerable overlap. There were also routes from skilled manual to 'whitecollar' status, particularly for skilled engineering workers who could move in to drafting or become marine engineering officers. It is worth noting that some manual workers in the inter war period, for example most rail and bus workers, would have at least as much guarantee of regular employment as some'whitecollar'Tyneside occupations. The employment of a railway signalman was much more regular than that of a Master Mariner in the depressed shipping industry. This issue of the location of social divisions is important and merits some theoretical discussion before we proceed with the empirical account.

## Cleavages Considered

A number of contemporary writers in urban sociology, particularly Saunders (1982,1985) have placed emphasis on what they describe as'new'social cleavages which have their origins not in the relationship of people to the process of production but rather in the way in which 'households' control assets. Of particular significance in this discussion has been the role of owner occupied houses as household assets. The focus on the household as a unit of 'consumption' is well taken, although it is much more sensible to consider households as involved with reproduction of labour power for most people rather than as mini-Versailles of conspicuous consumption. Likewise owner occupied houses are important as sources of wealth possession. Indeed the development of owner occupation as a tenure is the major factor in the modification of the distribution of 'marketable wealth' in the United Kingdom (see Royal Commission on the Distribution of Income and Wealth 1977) and the owner occupied dwelling represents the major element in the marketable wealth of most households.

Pahl has also discussed social differentiation, albeit in a rather more tentative and empirically based way. He has commented (1985) on the distinction between 'work rich' and 'work poor' households, a distinction which describes the relationship of households to the labour market in terms of the 'amount' of work they have access to. This distinction is sensible but needs elaboration. Economists have long used the term 'human capital' in discussing the role of skills in economic growth and rate of return analysis of personal investment treats time and money spent on one's own education as an investment like any other (see Blaug,1967). The distinction between skilled and semi/unskilled workers has generally been regarded as fundamental in understanding the nature of divisions within the working class. Clearly skills/capacities whether transferable as with craft/professional or employer specific (railway workers, civil servants) have resulted in differential rewards in the form of wages. Indeed a key source of wartime discontent between 1914 and 1918 was the way in which wartime regulation of labour trapped skilled workers with particular employers thereby preventing them moving for higher wages, with the consequence that unskilled and semi skilled wages moved closer to skilled.

In Tyneside's engineering industries the skill content was high and wages were also high in periods of work. Miners' wages were linked with coal prices, at least in the medium term, and shifted with market conditions. Evidence from the wage tables suggests that engineering workers in work were much more able to hold up wages and in any event the 1930s saw such a deflation in commodity prices, including the cost of housing, that real wages for regularly employed workers rose despite for example cuts in the salaries of public employees in 1931. What we need to look at is how position in the labour market shapes access to 'reproductive' resources, which may become the basis of asset ownership. The Paynes using an explicitly Weberian framework asserted (1978) that the connection between wages and housing was one of, and quite possibly the, major ways in which labour market position was translated into life chances. Although the terms carry a different burden Friedman's distinction between central and peripheral workers (1979) has something of the same implication. Position does not just determine (in Williams'sense of setting limits, 1982) immediate circumstances. It has important implications for potential. Indeed it may be that this 'potential' aspect, the effect of people's ability to organize their futures, is the most important aspect of the relationship between (again using Williams' terms) social being and social consciousness.

An examination of the introduction of 'cheap' working class accessible owner occupation in the inter-war years is of particular interest because the system as it developed then played a large part in the effective pre-emption of subsequent choices about housing tenure patterns in Britain. Dickens et al (1985) remind us of the importance of not assuming that the systems we have are the only ones possible. In Sweden most of the sorts of people who live in owner occupied dwellings in the UK live in co-operative housing which has very different implications for wealth accumulation. The development of a systems of owner occupation was not inevitable. Indeed evidence from the 1930s in particular suggests that it was very much a second choice for many who entered it. However the significance of tenure in relation to social divisions is great, if complex. To understand the social action which produced mass owner occupation we need first to consider the nature of the housing production system in the inter war period.

Getting Houses Built And Paid For.

The process of urban housing development requires four things. There must be land, which is expensive. There has to be a building production process which has considerable labour and material inputs and is also expensive. There must be customers to purchase the finished product, which incorporating as it does expensive land, labour and materials is very expensive. Finally there must be a credit system to advance the money needed to buy land, pay wages and materials costs and, given the very high costs of houses in relation to average earnings (although this ratio was at its historic low point in the 1930s it was still of the order of 3:1), there must be a system of consumer credit. There was nothing new here which emerged in relation to owner occupation. The system of relating land, production, customer and credit had been put together as the basis of providing dwellings for landlords to rent as a business. With owner occupation all that changed was the customer at the end of the process. As the Inland Revenue recognized, and as economists of all shades of political opinion agree, owner occupiers rent the dwelling to themselves and take an income in kind. Until 1963 this income was taxed in the UK as it still is in many other countries.

People owned houses for two reasons. Houses generate a flow of income, either as cash rents or kind accommodation. They also are speculative assets - they may increase in value at a rate greater than the general rate of inflation. Given the old fashioned nature of the housing production process, this is normally likely and the land element increases this speculative possibility. When the first version of this paper was written it was necessary to point out with some care that house prices do not inevitably rise. That care is no longer necessary. Certainly prices did not rise in the inter-war period. First, land was not a problem. There were limited planning constraints on urban sprawl and new transport technologies made much more land available for development. Second the inter war years did see major technological innovations in housing production. The result was that house prices generally fell in both money and real terms. This was particularly marked as between 1919-22 and the rest of the period but speculative gains were not a possibility at any time. The contemporary advantage of owner occupation is that it is not taxed but subsidized. Tax relief on mortgage interest is a perfectly legitimate business expense if landlords and owner occupiers are taxed on the income they get from owning houses. In the inter war period both were, at approximately the same rate, because owneroccupiers were taxed through Schedule A on the imputed real income they derived from living in their own house. In other words they were treated as if they rented the house to themselves. There was broad tenure neutrality between private renting and owner occupation. Both were eligible for lump sum subsidies for small houses under the 1919 Additional Powers and 1923 Chamberlain legislation. Both were taxed on real incomes. Owner occupiers did not have to pay the Landlords 'profit' but this can in part be regarded as a fee for the bother of having to manage the property in terms of organization of repairs,insurance etc. In the 1980s we were so used to making money from owner occupation that it was hard to realize that this is not inherent in the nature of the tenure but rather reflects land shortages and taxation systems. Now we are learning this the hard way.

The only advantageously subsidized system in the inter-war years was council housing and even here the subsidies under the 1919 and 1924 acts (the measures which related to general needs rather than the facilitating of slum clearance and relief of overcrowding) were of the same order in real terms as the capitalized lump sum payments to the private sector. The obvious question is why did private renting cease to deliver after 1919 on the scale on which it had delivered pre-1914 ? The obvious answer is rent control, not in actuality because new construction was always exempt under the rent acts, but the threat of its implementation. Why invest in something where controls could be applied when there were alternatives available ? Confidence did recover in private renting and a good deal of 1930s construction was sold to private landlords, but the qualms were well founded because rent control was reintroduced in September 1939 and it was this second phase which finished that tenure as a source of new provision. It is worth noting that central government did constantly try to revive private renting through a series of measures directed at reducing the extent of rent control (see Beirne, 1979). The notion that the urban petit-bourgeoisie were sacrificed as expressed by Daunton (1984) seems misguided. Local studies of the kind represented by this paper show that it was not so much a matter of the urban petit-bourgeoisie being sacrificed as of the more advanced elements of that group proving highly adaptable at manipulating possiblilities provided by central legislation and creating a new role in relation to facilitating owner occupation.

The key to the whole issue of housing provision is borrowing. Local authorities could borrow easily, if let by central government. Loan sanction powers were introduced in order to regulate the rush of borrowing under the 1919 Addison Act but despite this control local authorities were of a scale to manage large debts. The private sector alternative was provided by the building society movement. As early as the 1870s the working class controlled terminating societies had been less important than the new permanent societies controlled by the urban bourgeoisie and acting as specialist housing banks, originally in relation to the system of private renting. Building societies could and did loan on land and builders' work in progress, but were most important as sources of funds for final purchasers. They represented a relatively safe investment - there had been some notorious failures pre 1914 (see Boddy 1978), but local societies lending in markets they knew, and to a considerable extent controlled, were generally secure.

There is a good deal of archive material available on Tyneside building societies. Two interesting ones are the Tynemouth Victoria and the South Shields Provincial. The first was the largest of the North Shields societies. The directors included builders and estate agents, some of whom at various times were members of the local authority. The common connection seems in large part to have been masonic. For example Captain Milburn, the society's Vice Chairman for many years and the former commodore of Knott's Prince Line, was according to his 1932 obituaries a prominent local Conservative, Wesleyan Methodist, teetotaller and Free Mason.The society advanced £3,500 as a mortgage on the Masonic Temple in Albion Road, North Shields but the bulk of its business in the inter war years was in medium priced new housing, for example in the Balkwell and Verne Road areas.

The historically dominant figures in the Shields Commercial were the Chapman family. These were prominent local Tories and accountants in South Shields (legend has it that the family's original occupation was as bumbailiffs) and their inter war representative played a major part in attempting to impose punitive conditions on poor relief. The family developed land for cheap owner occupation in Harton in the 1920s and 30s, although much of the loan finance to purchasers came from another local society. In 1936 the Shields Commercial, again the largest locally, had assets of £683,000 of which £670,000 were in the form of mortgages. The average of the 1306 mortgages was £513. There were infact 1019 mortgages of less than £500, 187 of £500 to £999, 83 of £1000 to £2999, 11 of £3000 to £4999 and 6 of £5000 or more. The larger mortgages would not necessarily have been on large single properties. Some would have been on blocks for private landlords. For example the Tynemouth Victoria had advanced £3500 to its solicitor F.H. Kidd in 1936 against six houses (probably in 12 flats) in Verne Road, North Shields.

The archive material for the Shields Commercial interestingly includes the Cash Book and Journal of R. Redhead of the prominent local shipbuilding family, a genuine local industrial capitalist. In 1936 Redhead made some £110,000 in investments. Some of this was dealing in a portfolio but clearly this was an unusual year because there were £75,000 receipts on life insurance policies. Of this total nearly £34,000 was invested in nine different local building societies. Other investments included £11,000 in clearing bank shares and £23,500 in insurance shares and policies. The remainder was placed in a range of utilities, railway and industrial investments. Clearly building societies were regarded by wealthy capitalists as a good bet.

Building societies were traditionally cautious in terms of the amount they would lend. Before the 1930s they would almost never advance more than about 70% of a valuation. This posed difficulties for builders and in the 30s nationally and locally a system of 'builders advances', i.e. deposits made by builders with the society as guarantees against the loan until the outstanding balance was reduced, became common. As we shall see this occurred on Tyneside. It is also worth noting that the development of the 'Builders Pools' of deposits extended the geographical range of lending of the societies. Thus in the 1930s the North and South Shields societies were lending on housing developments in Sunderland, Rowlands Gill, West Hartlepool and Liverpool, as well as on Tyneside.

The builders of the inter-war years are worthy of attention in their own right. Although there had been large builders in the pre 1914 period (see North Tyneside CDP 1977, Benwell CDP 1978) the developer had predominated. Developers were usually quite large capitalists or landowners who laid out large areas of land for building estates and then sold off building plots. The homogeneous character of pre 1914 Tyneside terraces is far more a function of covenants attached to site purchases by land developers than of the streets being built by the same builder. Indeed small developments of two or three houses (or pairs of flats) seem to have been the rule rather than the exception. In the inter war period the same process continued but there was a far greater tendency to combine the role of developer and builder, especially in the 1930s. Indeed the main facilitators of small scale builders using developed sites seem to have been the local authorities, for example Tynemouth CB on sites at the Balkwell, Hunts Hill and in Cullercoats (see Byrne 1980).

Examples of larger developer builders are provided by Chapman in South Shields whose developments in the Harton area are an example of a traditional bourgeois land developer taking on the building role, and by Leech at Benwell and Walker where the techniques of the very large builder developer of the kind which was to dominate post war owner occupied suburbanization were put together on a medium scale. A good example of scale is provided by the operations of E. P.Calderwood on the Chowdene estate in Low Fell (in an area which was originally outside Gateshead CB boundary). The local press in the mid 1930s (Gateshead Cuttings) referred to more than 800 dwellings having been built in this area in less than ten years. Calderwood had built over 350 and was planning to build another 200.The total investment by the builder was some £300,000. The 1935 Gateshead Official Guide described the consequences of such development:

> "In the Low Fell district ... this development of land for housing purposes has been most marked and there has sprung up a large number of semi-detached villas of an attractive type... There has been, and is, a great demand for these houses, as quickly as construction is completed, and many of the people who tenant them have moved there from Newcastle where they find their vocation. Gateshead, in fact, is rapidly becoming a residential suburb of Newcastle."

The scale of these developments in the four county boroughs is indicated by the housing completion figures in Table 1.

**TABLE 1**

**HOUSING CONSTRUCTION IN TYNESIDE COUNTY BOROUGHS IN THE INTER WAR YEARS**

| | 1920-1930 | 1931-1940 |
|---|---|---|
| South Shields | | |
| Social Housing | 1466 | 2949 |
| Private with subsidy | 414 | 0 |
| Private without subsidy | 314 | 2370 |
| Newcastle | | |
| Social Housing | 5678 | 6516 |
| Private with subsidy | | |
| Private without subsidy | 3325 | 12646 |
| Gateshead | | |
| Social Housing | 1379 | 1705 |
| Private with subsidy | 725 | 0 |
| Private without subsidy | 436 | 2913 |
| Tynemouth | | |
| Social Housing | 924 | 2542 |
| Private with subsidy | 984 | 0 |
| Private without subsidy | 468 | 2662 |

Social Housing is Council Housing plus North East Housing Association.

Source - Annual Reports of Medical Officers of Health. These did not differentiate between subsidised and unsubsidised construction for Newcastle City.

A good deal of suburban development in fact went on beyond original borough boundaries. Both Benwell and Walker were originally separate urban districts which were added to Newcastle City and Harton was a separate district which was added to South Shields. Gateshead expanded south to take in part of Lamesly parish at Chowdene. However a good deal of development went on in what remained separate districts, particularly in Gosforth, Whitley Bay and to a lesser extent in Cleadon Village in Boldon.

## Housing The Aristocracy Of Labour

If we consider the housing aspirations of the social groups who gained access to new owner occupied housing in the inter war period, we can identify five possible methods through which they might have gained housing of this kind. These are through high quality council housing as represented by the 1920s construction, through the system of owner occupation as it did develop, through an employer led system, through a worker led system or through housing co-operatives on the continental model. Price in his fascinating discussion of 'the rise and fall of council housing in South Shields 1914-1932' (1982) shows that all except the last were possible options in that town in the 1920s. Thus the local authority under Labour pressure built the Cleadon Park estate for renting although a move was made by Smith's Dock company to acquire the land for its workers exclusively. In 1923 with the support of the majority of the Labour members the local authority sold some 290 of the houses it had built to rent. In 1924 the authority advanced capital to the St Hilda's Miners lodge for an assisted purchase scheme by the lodge's members. This was abandoned when the responsible lodge secretary was sacked by his lodge and became a founder member of the 'Durham and Northumberland Miners Non-Political Union' (Price pp28-9). Price has an interesting discussion of the local authority sales. He contends that:

> "It was widely acknowledged that the housing shortage was so chronic as to be indifferent to occupational divisions within the working class. It was simply not true to say that people unable to buy would not suffer any harm by remaining where they were. Artisans and white-collar workers were themselves likely, although not perhaps as likely as others, to be living in overcrowded, over-priced and insanitary accommodation."
>
> The Moderate coalition was in fact correct in arguing that under prevailing conditions it made little difference whether the houses were let or sold, the occupants would be much the same people. "(1982, pp 27-8).

In fact as Price himself indicates (p29) nearly half of potential purchasers had not been on the housing waiting list and an inspection of 162 of the 293 conveyances for the sales (Tyne Wear County Archives) shows that the purchasers did not come from sanitarily inadequate slums.

Contemporary debate at the national level certainly did not automatically uphold the desirability of owner occupation. Instead in the 1930s there was a very clear assertion that people would rather be tenants. For example a chairman of the Building Societies Association claimed:

> "The new owner occupiers were so by necessity rather than choice... The main source of the increased demand for buildings society mortgages came from people forced to become owner occupiers because there were no houses to let."
>
> (Walter Harvey quoted in Boddy, 1980 p15)

Local support for this position is provided by the more than 2,000 applications for 35 houses built by Gateshead CBC at Field House Lane in 1929-30. These high quality and high rent dwellings were all delayed representation of Wheatley Act style construction and very different from the slum clearance stock at Old Fold and elsewhere which was to succeed them.

What is clear is that by the 1930s the easiest way to get a decent modern dwelling was to buy it. The local authorities were no longer building for general needs and the quality and social reputation of the slum clearance replacement estates was low. There was indeed a revival of private landlord provision. Most of this was in 1930s versions of Tyneside flats, an interesting parallel with the flatted construction of very similar design on slum clearance estates. However while this was modern in terms of facilities, the flats were poky. Some of the houses being built were purchased by landlords for letting. In South Shields the Provincial Building society granted a series of mortgages on houses at Harton Rise built by Chapman. Of 32 mortgages granted in this area in the Autumn of 1933, there were five 'doubles' for two properties each. These are houses so landlords were buying at least one extra as an investment. Interestingly the 'landlord purchasers' included a fitter and motor driver in addition to more obvious landlords. Chapman deposited £24 security against advances of £374 on valuations of £405 for about half of these properties, but not in any of the multiple purchases. Purchasers were a mixture in about equal parts of white collar workers, skilled manual workers and persons whose occupations were not given.

In 1936 this society made a number of advances against properties being built by Messrs Leech in Walker and Benwell. Typically these were advances of £320 on properties which were sold on 99 year leases. In many cases Leech made security deposits. In 1933 Leech's were advertising properties for sale in Walker in the local press at 14/6d weekly with a small deposit for a 3 bedroomed semi with bath, living room and kitchenette (Evening Chronicle 29th June 1933). This squares with building society indications of prices and repayment costs. Most of the advances in Walker were to skilled workers with rather fewer going to white collar workers. At this time typical private sector rents were 12/6d per week inclusive of rates for a three roomed unmodernized flat in Heaton, 13/6d inclusive for a four roomed upstairs unmodernized flat with skullery in Second Ave Heaton, 18/6d for a self contained house with bathroom in Falmouth Rd and about 11/6d (North Shields) to 15/7d (South Shields) for parlour council houses with two to four bedrooms. Price (1982, p33) shows that Cleadon Park Estate rents in South Shields ranged from 11/6d to 14/- inclusive of rates in 1930 whilst the cost of buying plus rates for the same properties in 1924 ranged from 15/4d to 18/5d. Correspondence in the local press (quoted in Byrne 1980 p184) suggested that in North Shields a £475 house could be bought at 12/9d per week on 20 years purchase net of rates. With rates this would total 16/- compared with good council housing renting at 11/6d inclusive. The owner occupiers would also have to pay for repairs and structural insurance. All in all owner occupation looked financially attractive against private renting but not against renting good council property.

The problem was that access to good council property was virtually impossible.

Where The Aristocracy Of Labour Lived In The 1930s

Ward's Directories for the inter-war years are a very useful source for this study because the street lists included occupational descriptions of heads of households. The listings are by no means complete. Not everyone even in the streets covered made a directory entry. Frequently no occupation was given. The directories generally did not get farther down market than the respectable working class areas and there were strange omissions - for example Harton Rise does not appear in South Shields. Nevertheless although there are many defects there is enough information to get a crude idea of what sort of people lived in what sort of housing. Table 2 is based on an inspection of the 1938 directory for 'respectable areas' in East Newcastle (Heaton, Walkergate and Walker), Gateshead (LowFell and Saltwell), North Shields (Balkwell, Verne Road and Chirton) and South Shields (Cauldwell, Harton and Cleadon Park). The housing selected is classified into three types viz. 1920s council housing, 1920s and 30s bottom of market owner occupied construction and pre 1914 'good'terraced flats and houses. It does not include slums or slum clearance replacement estates which were not generally covered by the directories. Neither does it include unequivocally middle class housing of a more expensive kind whether pre or post 1914. The coverage is of the middle part of the system. Sampling was quasi random by street with all records for a street taken. This gives a representative account of patterns. Heads of house holds were classified as 'white collar/shopkeeper', 'skilled manual', 'other manual'and 'other'. The last was those where no occupation was given and was about half female.

**TABLE 2**

**CLASS OF HOUSEHOLD HEAD AND TENURE IN 1938**

| Tenure Type | % White Collar Shopkeeper | % Skilled Manual | % Unskilled | % Other | Numbers | Numbers Possible |
|---|---|---|---|---|---|---|
| South Shields | | | | | | |
| Owner Occupied | 57 | 23 | 1 | 19 | 111 | 114 |
| Council | 22 | 51 | 5 | 22 | 306 | 397 |
| Pre 1914 | 31 | 37 | 3 | 29 | 487 | 626 |
| East Newcastle | | | | | | |
| Owner Occupied | 38 | 38 | 2 | 22 | 307 | 366 |
| Council | 18 | 54 | 7 | 20 | 257 | 287 |
| Pre 1914 | 18 | 41 | 11 | 30 | 363 | 459 |
| Gateshead | | | | | | |
| Owner Occupied | 39 | 26 | 2 | 32 | 211 | 250 |
| Council | 22 | 45 | 3 | 30 | 179 | 226 |
| Pre 1914 | 23 | 46 | 9 | 21 | 170 | 291 |
| North Shields | | | | | | |
| Owner Occupied | 33 | 39 | 3 | 24 | 243 | 302 |
| Council | 29 | 47 | 11 | 13 | 105 | 157 |
| Pre 1914 | 20 | 40 | 6 | 34 | 233 | 310 |

The procedure was crude but there are enough cases for a very obvious pattern to emerge. In all four areas the most white collar housing type was the 'owner occupied' (some of which would be rented). However in all four towns a significant proportion of heads of households in the owner occupied areas were skilled workers and in East Newcastle and North Shields there were as many or more skilled heads of households as there were white collar/shopkeepers. It has to be stressed that 'whitecollar/ shopkeeper' means exactly that. These people were teachers, clerks, grocers, draughtsmen, merchant navy officers and policemen. There were no doctors or solicitors. Skilled manual includes foremen. Skilled manual predominated in the other two sorts of housing but there were significant numbers of white collar/shopkeepers. It is particularly notable that in the 1920s council housing this category was far larger in all four towns than that of 'other manual' (ie. semi and unskilled occupations). Indeed the 'non-aristocrats' of labour scarcely figure at all in in any of these types of tenure/locations in inter-war Tyneside.

The pattern of occupation-tenure had distinct political relations. All four of the Tyneside county boroughs were under non-Labour control for large parts of the inter-war years. Indeed Tynemouth CB as such was never controlled outright by Labour and Labour never won control of Newcastle until the late 1950s. Even South Shields and Gateshead were not all that safe for Labour until quite recently. South Shields CB was under non Labour control in the early 70s and Gateshead was only retained by the aldermanic vote. Labour's wards in urban Tyneside, as opposed to the coalfield, in the inter-war period were of two types. First Labour generally held the inner city slums. Second it held council housing areas including the good council housing of the 1920s. However areas like Heaton and Saltwell, ie good pre 1914 housing, were either safe Tory (or some local disguise like 'Progressive' in South Shields) or marginal until quite recently, and the owner occupied areas were Tory (or proxy) until the 1970s. The political relations of tenure had been well understood by anti-socialist political forces at both the national and local level. The withdrawal of good council housing from the white collar and skilled working class in the 1930s was quite explicitly motivated in considerable part by the intention of winning these social groups away from socialism, and a precisely similar strategy under lay the repeat performance when general needs housing provision was abandoned in favour of slum clearance replacement in the middle 1950s.

## Class And Owner Occupation.

The relationship between housing tenure and political behaviour is of great importance in understanding how developments in social reproduction affect the forms of class action. However the development of working class owner occupation also had very direct material advantages for the urban bourgeoisie. That social group's intensely active support for private housing development is yet another vivid historical illustration of the reality of 'instrumental' use being made of the state, and of the continuation of this beyond the period described by Barke and Calcott in this volume. A fascinating account of the actual 'modes' through which this was mediated remains to be written as history, particularly for the 1950s and subsequently, although a cursory survey of novelists as diverse as Jack Common or John Braine will provide a good account of the role of Masons, Golf Club and Conservative Club. What is interesting is a consideration of the sources of hostility to council housing. This seems to have had two aspects. One was the hostility of private landlords to a competitor which provided better quality at lower rents, this is discussed in Byrne(1980). What also seems very important, and which the present author had not recognized for this period until carrying out the research on which this study is based, was the issue of land development gains.

It is vital to recognize that unless the building industry is nationalized or municipalized (direct labour), and it was not to any very great extent in this period in the North East - certainly not by the 1930s- it makes little difference to a builder as an industrial capitalist whether he (usually) builds for owner occupation or on tender for a local authority. The difference in profitability comes not from the construction process, (although of course local authorities were and are able to exercise quality control at all stages of the production process in a way in which a purchaser for owner occupation is not), but from land. Local authority development was and is almost invariably on land owned by the authority in the first place. The big money in private urban development comes from acquiring agricultural sites and turning them into housing land. It was this which betterment levy etc in post war planning legislation was designed to tax, but there was no such provision in any real sense in the inter war years. This alone provided quite enough incentive for urban bourgeois hostility and obstruction in relation to good quality council housing.

The advantage of development for owner occupation as opposed to private renting was that it invariably led to a quick realization of such development gains. This was recognized by contemporary critics, for example Walter Harvey, later Chairman of the Building Societies Association, who argued that:

> "The profits of housebuilders and landowners are in many instances unconscionable and responsibility attaches to the societies that makes them possible....(the societies)... were drawn off financing the building of houses to let by the....much more profitable business of financing house purchase at scarcity prices, mainly for the benefit of the builder-seller." (quoted Boddy, 1980, p15)

The process described here laid the foundations for the central element in Britain's housebuilding industry of today, the large developer builder.

However, despite contemporary complaints about 'gerry building' the customers did not get a bad deal in the long run. What has mattered in that long run is the form of social differentiation associated with different tenures. This is rather more complicated on Tyneside than it is in many British cities, precisely because Tyneside has so much good council housing. The similarities in social composition between cheap inter war owner occupied areas and 1920s council housing have already been demonstrated. The very good quality housing built between 1945 and the early 1950s was if anything even more desirable than the 20s stock, and in any event it was the only new working class housing available in this period. If that pattern of provision had continued things would have been very different today. Instead we had a reversion to the social divisions of the 30s with the post 1955 abandonment of council house building for general needs.

In the 1930s the social structure of Tyneside was clear. At the bottom was a clearly differentiated group of the poor who were low skilled and or benefit dependent. These lived in slums or in 1930s slum replacement estates like the Deans in South Shields or Old Fold in Gateshead. At the top were the rich bourgeoisie and professionals who lived in large private houses. In between were the white collar and skilled/employed working class who lived in good terraces, good council housing and the new cheap owner occupied stock. There were far sharper downward divisions for this group than there were upward divisions. Indeed it can be argued that the development of working class owner occupation was vital to the sharpening of these divisions. Burnett has observed of inter war speculative housing that :

> "...the new recruits almost always entered the class at the bottom, and the growth of numbers was, therefore, mainly downwards into categories of occupation and income which only just qualified for admission." (1986, p251)

This point does not seem to have been properly appreciated by Swenarton and Taylor (1985) who generally dismiss the importance of working class owner occupation in the interwar years arguing that :

> "At the time of what few would argue was its greatest phase of expansion, it seems that the class composition of owner occupation did change, but scarcely in the way suggeted by the theory of the 'ramparts' (against socialism) strategy. By 1938 owner-occupation had become, not less middle class, less, not more working class. If any class was sucessfully incorporated by owner-occupation in this period, it was not the working class".(p392)

Swenarton and Taylor's argument is based on nationally available evidence. However the quality, or rather relevance, of this is somewhat suspect. For example they reproduce a table taken from Minutes of Evidence to Departmental Committee on Valuation for Rates (1939) on the weekly outgoings associated with houses of various prices. The lowest outgoing given is £1-0-5d, but this is for a house costing between £500 and £600. The dwellings being dealt with in this paper cost around £400. Thus Swenarton and Taylor's extension of the argument also falls :

> "According to the Ministry of Labour's 1931 survey, 81% of the working class (those earning £3 per week or less) could afford no more than 12s per week on housing and only 2% could afford anything more than 14s, assuming that no more than one fifth of weekly earnings could be spent on housing. The conclusion seems to be that in general only the elite of

the working class could afford home ownership - and even then only at the cost of self-sacrifice and thrift". (1986, p392)

There are three faults here. First much of the housing was cheap enough to come close to the 14s cost. Second the £3 per week cut off is an arbitrary statisticians' device rather than any theoretically grounded definition of being working class. By definition a lot of workers would be earning a bit more than this, i.e. between £3 and £4 (given the invariable shape of any income distribution). Third, the situation in the mid 1930s, the real period of expansion, was very different for household incomes from the situation in 1931. Real incomes had risen quite substantially for those in work. This is why Waites were able to build in London for the postman, bus driver and railway employees within walking distance of a tube station using regularly employed construction workers who lived within cycling distance of the site (Ambrose, 1985).

This is yet another illustration of the absolute necessity in housing history of going to the locality. Contemporary national impressions of the situation were frequently plain wrong. However, the argument is one of degree rather than substance. It is clear that in the 1930s some (I would say quite a lot) of workers were gaining access to owner-occupation, not necessarily as a result of choice but because they could not get a modern rented house. What resulted was an earlier version of what is now called' the two thirds-one third society' although the extent of unemployment on Tyneside was such until the outbreak of war that it was closer to a half and half society. That societal war and full employment were to produce very different housing consequences. What is interesting is the close resemblance of social arrangements in the mean and nasty 1980s to those of the mean and nasty 1930s. What must be emphasized about the development of owner occupation for working class people is that it was neither inevitable nor accidental. In a period when it was not a very good deal financially it was imposed, but the consequences are with us today.

DAVID BYRNE

**Plates 11 and 12.**
Edwardian villas often occupied by Labour aristocrats.
Plate 11 (above), Dryden Road, Low Fell.
Plate 12 (below), Musgrave Garden City, Durham Road, Gateshead.

**Plate 13.**
Lobley Hill, 1930s. This development continued the tradition of home ownership for skilled workers.

**Plate 14.**
The municipal alternative to working class home ownership.
"Homes fit for Heroes", council houses of the 1920s. Sheriff's Hill, Gateshead.

## References


Beirne P., 1977, Fair Rent and Legal Fiction, Macmillan.

Benwell CDP, 1980, Private Housing and the Working Class.

Blaug M., 1967, The Economics of Education, Penguin.

Boddy M., 1980, The Building Societies, Macmillan.

Burnett J., 1986, A Social History of Housing, Methuen.

Byrne D S., 1980, 'The standard of council housing in inter-war North Shields' in Melling J., (Ed).

Byrne D S 1982, 'Class and the local state' in International Journal of Urban and Regional Research Vol. 6, No.1

Byrne D S et al, 1985, Housing and Health, Gower.

Damer S., 1980, 'State, Class and Housing' in Melling J., (Ed)

Dickens, P., et al, 1985, Housing, States and Localities, Heinmann.

Gilbert B., 1970, British Social Policy 1919-1939, Batsford.


## Primary Sources


Medical Officers' of Health Annual Reports 1919-39

City of Newcastle.
County Borough of Gateshead.
County Borough of South Shields.
County Borough of Tynemouth.

Wards Director - Newcastle and District 1938

Tyne & Wear County Archives

File 497 S Camborn and Sons - Adverts 1939-70

File 482 - Shields Commercial Building Society

File 497 - Tynemouth Victoria Building Society

File 518 - Newcastle and Gateshead Building Society


## Secondary Sources


Gregory D., & Urry J., (Eds), 1985, Social Relations and Spatial Structures, Macmillan.

Karn V & Ungerson C., 1980, The Consumer Experience of Housing, Gower.

Manders F., 1974, A History of Gateshead, Gateshead CBC.

Melling J. (Ed), 1980, Housing Social Policy and the State, Croom Helm.

North Tyneside CDP, 1977, North Shields : Working Class Politics and Housing 1900-1977.

Pahl R., 1985, 'The restructuring of capital, the local political economy and household work strategies' in Gregory D., and Urry J., (Eds).

Payne G., & Payne J., 1978, 'Housing Pathways and Stratification' in Journal of Social Policy Vol.6 No.2

Price D., 1982, Fighting like Tigers : the rise and fall of council housing in South Shields, Newcastle Polytechnic

Swennarton M. 1981, Homes fit for heroes Heinmann

Swennarton M and Taylor S. 'The scale and nature of the growth of owner occupation in Britain between the Wars', Economic History Review, No.1, 1985.

Saunders P., 1982, 'Beyond Housing Classes; Working Papers in Urban and Regional Studies 35 University of Sussex.

Saunders P., 1985, 'Space, the City and Urban Sociology' in Gregor D., and Urry J., (Eds)

Williams R., 1982, Problems in Materialism and Culture, Verso.

## MEADOWELL AND MYTHOLOGY: THE MAKING OF A 'PROBLEM ESTATE'

### Introduction

As with all other British conurbations, Tyneside includes within its boundaries that particular category of working class housing that has come to be known as the 'problem estate'. This chapter examines the history of one such area, the Meadowell council estate in North Shields, now located within the local authority area of the North Tyneside Metropolitan Borough Council. The chapter is concerned with the physical development and evolution of the area but more particularly with the less tangible, but ultimately more potent, feature of the estate's reputation. A re-examination of these issues is especially timely as the estate is now assured a particular place in the history and mythology of working class housing on Tyneside, a place based upon specific recent events which appear to have confirmed local 'folk-knowledge' that the area is indeed a 'problem estate' inhabited by 'problem people'. However, a central thesis of this chapter is that 'label' and 'reality' have not always been so convergent and that such convergence has, to a considerable extent, been 'manufactured'. The estate was seen in a particular (negative) light from its initial construction but this bore only a limited relation to reality. This negative perception owed much to the combination of local and wider processes operating at the time of construction. The latter relates especially to the national 'ethos' surrounding the legislation leading to the development of slum clearance estates; the former relates to the local interpretation and implementation of that legislation and the specific circumstances of the local housing market at the time of construction. These factors created an environment which made it almost impossible for the Meadowell estate to be seen in anything other than a negative light, regardless of objective reality. Against this background, we should perhaps not be surprised if, two generations on, a considerable degree of convergence of label and reality has taken place, a convergence which the events of September, 1991 appear to confirm.

On the evening of Monday September 9, 1991 the Meadowell council estate in North Shields experienced an outbreak of civil disturbance, reported in both the local and national media as a 'riot'. This was followed by similar events in the west end of Newcastle upon Tyne on 11-13 September, resulting in 323 people, mainly youths, being arrested in North Shields and Newcastle upon Tyne by 28 September. These disturbances on Tyneside had, in turn, followed quickly upon the heels of riots in Oxford and Cardiff. Inevitably, parallels were sought with the major urban riots of 1981 but real similarities are difficult to find. The riots of 1981 had a much more explicit racial context than those of 1991 and issues concerned with racist policing of inner city areas were never far from the surface of events at that time. Ostensibly, if a common thread existed between the disturbances of 1991 it appeared to be found in car related crime and the mis-named 'joy-riding' phenomenon. However, any similarity amongst the disturbances of 1991 is purely superficial and, certainly in the case of Meadowell, the roots of the disturbances lie at a much deeper level. The two sets of riots, separated by a decade, also had different 'targets'. In 1981 the principal target was, of course, the police and, secondly, the manifestations of conspicuous consumption in areas neighbouring the riot streets were looted for consumer items such as videos. In 1991 the communities' own facilities were, tragically, the all too frequent targets (Campbell, 1991). Schools, community centres, local small shops and post offices were amongst such local facilities burnt, destroyed or badly damaged.

The fact that the 'targets' for the riots should change over a decade is not without significance. The riots in both 1981 and 1991 were located either in inner city areas or in so-called 'problem estates'. The locales were therefore similar, being the residential areas of the deprived, the underclass, or whatever other 'social science' term is appropriate for those who fail to benefit from economic growth within the wider society. Yet, whereas in 1981 the frustrations and anger felt were directed externally, in 1991 such emotions were, to a much greater degree, directed internally. It is difficult not to feel that this is one manifestation of a significant and, sadly, negative change in the self-perception of at least a proportion of young people in such areas. Such areas are not immune from external events and it is arguable that a decade of increasing personal wealth for many has led to a sharpening of social differentials, that a proportion of the 'underclass' in inner city areas and 'problem estates' now live in households where few have ever worked and where there is no prospect of ever working but, more importantly, where 'society' tells them that such a situation is their own fault. The last decade has seen a significant 'hardening' of social attitudes at the same time as wealth and welfare divisions have grown. The self-perception of many young people in the 'problem estates' therefore cannot fail to be influenced by such messages. If one is constantly told that the 'fault' of your own poverty, unemployment etc. lies within yourself or your own community then we should perhaps not be surprised when young people turn, at least partially, upon their own communities to commit acts of vandalism, hooliganism and arson against their neighbours. Thus, the riots of 1991 signalled, to some extent, the estrangement of many youths from their own communities.

Not only is a significant proportion of young men marginalised in the contemporary labour market, they are increasingly marginalised within their own communities (Turnbull, forthcoming). Many such youths are ".. economic victims who were not only a product of alienation; they produced it." (Campbell, op. cit, p.21).

Although these issues arise from contemporary events, it is the contention of the authors of this chapter that they cannot be divorced from the past. The Meadowell estate, and especially South Meadowell, has consistently been characterised as a 'problem estate', both in the academic literature and in the local, popular imagination:

> "...one of the most notoriously problematic Tyneside council estates is the South Meadowell in North Tyneside, an estate of mostly flats, built to reduced standards in the 1930s to rehouse the population of the riverside slums of North Shields."

(Cameron and Crompton, 1988).

Underlying such descriptions, although not always explicitly stated, is the view that Meadowell (formerly 'The Ridges') has always been a problem estate. As we shall see, such a view has been implicit in most of the interpretations of the history of Meadowell. Furthermore, this perception of the area carries with it the implication of a 'natural' sequence of events, leading from the way the estate was initially built and peopled, through the development of maintenance, allocation and social problems, and culminating in the 'riots' of September 1991. Residents of other parts of North Tyneside made comments such as the following to the authors after the 'riots': "I'm only surprised it hasn't happened there before.", "What else do you expect from that scum?" and, in more liberal vein, "Have you seen the state of that estate? I'm not sure I blame them really."

Thus there is an implied feeling that the recent disturbances on Meadowell were inevitable, almost a product of 'natural' evolution although, in this case, the evolution took the form of a downward spiral. One of the purposes of this chapter is to challenge this assumption. To imply that significant civil disturbance was somehow inevitably the end result of Meadowell's position as a 'problem estate' from its initial construction and subsequently is to distort reality. In particular such an interpretation gives too much significance to the internal character of the estate in terms of its design and its people. These things are, of course, important but equally significant is the external social, political and economic environment which constantly shifts and changes and which partially governs the way in which specific areas are viewed and changes the roles they play. Such areas are, of course, largely defined in terms of comparisons with other areas but that is rather different from the argument being developed here, that changes within the external environment itself influence the way such places are seen and therefore the 'labels' they acquire, possibly regardless of any change within the areas themselves. Subsequently, the internal dynamic of such places becomes susceptible to influence from these external forces. Yet, in the history of Meadowell its problems have almost always been internalised. Thus although the history of the Meadowell estate is well documented, this chapter seeks to place this particular working class housing development in a wider context and to argue that there was nothing inherently 'inevitable' in the area becoming the perceived problem that it has. Indeed, we can argue that Meadowell came very rapidly to be seen as a problem because it was ideologically necessary for many people to see it as such.

Meadowell: a 'Problem Estate'?

Most contemporary empirical data would appear to suggest South Meadowell exhibits many characteristics of a problem estate. Figure 1 shows the proportion of the tenants of each council estate in North Tyneside who wished to move elsewhere. This represents a useful indication of the popularity of an estate with its residents as obviously discontented tenants will wish to transfer to another area. It is clear that the less popular estates tend to be concentrated along the riverside, and that South Meadowell is the least popular estate with its own residents at this time with some 23% wishing to transfer elsewhere.

Table 1 gives some indication of the standing of South Meadowell in relation to North Tyneside's other large estates (30 in number). In addition to being the 'worst' estate in terms of desire to move elsewhere, South Meadowell is also the 'worst' of these larger estates in terms of the level of sales under the 'Right to Buy' legislation (no houses had been sold on the estate at this time), the level of turnover as indicated by the proportion of the tenants who have lived on the estate for less than 10 years, and the proportion of lone parent families. It is the second worst estate in terms of overcrowding, and the third worst in terms of car ownership and the level of vandalism. It is the eighth worst in terms of the level of voids on the estate. However, it is ranked eighth 'best' in terms of the proportion of the properties that have been modernised.

From this evidence it would appear that the perception of South Meadowell as a problem estate is justified. Yet, this may be questioned. A review of the concepts and literature on this issue indicates that the case of South Meadowell does not fit neatly into any of the widely recognised theories of the origins of problem estates.

The identification of so-called problem estates has generated a growing literature containing reference to a variety of processes which may be instrumental in producing such problem areas (see, for example, Baldwin, 1975). Three main groups of theories may be identified. One theme recognised in a number of studies concerns the so-called 'dumping' of problem tenants in specific areas by local housing authorities. Council tenants, both existing residents, and those who are perceived as 'problems' are therefore helpless victims of allocation policies adopted by urban managers (Gill,1977; Gray,1976). However, it is likely that through time the estate will acquire a bad reputation, become difficult to let - especially to 'decent' tenants - and the relative concentration of problem households is likely to increase. Housing managers become increasingly negative in their perception of such areas and this strongly influences their future allocation strategies (Taylor and Hadfield, 1982). Thus a downward spiral sets in and is perpetuated over time (English, 1979).

**TABLE 1**

**COMPARISON OF SOUTH MEADOWELL AND OTHER LARGE ESTATES IN NORTH TYNESIDE ON SEVEN INDICATORS, 1985.**

| Estate | % Sales | % FullCentHt. | % Vand | % 0-10yrs | % NoCar | % SPFms | % Crwd 1981 |
|---|---|---|---|---|---|---|---|
| Killingworth | 7.6 | 22.4 | 9.2 | 76.1 | 61.5 | 6.0 | 3.2 |
| Burradon | 14.8 | 65.2 | 2.4 | 44.5 | 67.0 | 2.6 | 4.6 |
| Dudley | 10.3 | 72.9 | 2.4 | 45.8 | 71.9 | 6.0 | 3.0 |
| WideOpen | 17.2 | 30.7 | 1.7 | 41.6 | 61.9 | 1.4 | 1.9 |
| ClousdenHill | 21.4 | 11.2 | 4.5 | 43.3 | 64.0 | 3.1 | 0.8 |
| Palmersville | 7.4 | 80.1 | 4.6 | 67.1 | 72.6 | 3.7 | 3.7 |
| Moorside | 7.4 | 96.2 | 6.7 | 37.2 | 65.9 | 3.2 | 3.0 |
| Seatonville | 20.0 | 78.4 | 1.1 | 25.5 | 64.3 | 3.3 | 4.5 |
| Hillheads | 13.6 | 98.8 | 1.0 | 23.7 | 70.1 | 2.4 | 4.6 |
| Broadway | 24.9 | 43.9 | 1.5 | 31.2 | 62.0 | 1.5 | 3.6 |
| Marden | 22.3 | 34.8 | 1.2 | 20.9 | 64.8 | 2.1 | 4.1 |
| Longbenton | 5.0 | 15.1 | 10.9 | 60.9 | 82.1 | 4.8 | 5.3 |
| GoathlandAve | 12.5 | 79.7 | 5.3 | 34.7 | 75.3 | 3.9 | 5.4 |
| BattleHill | 13.4 | 99.9 | 6.1 | 53.7 | 64.8 | 6.6 | 7.7 |
| HighHowden | 10.4 | 37.3 | 6.3 | 48.4 | 75.2 | 4.2 | 5.3 |
| Rosehill | 8.3 | 73.5 | 5.7 | 58.8 | 81.4 | 4.4 | 3.9 |
| N.Meadowell | 0.8 | 15.9 | 8.0 | 68.3 | 85.3 | 6.2 | 8.6 |
| Balkwell | 6.8 | 0.8 | 1.3 | 47.2 | 79.0 | 3.2 | 3.6 |
| W.Chirton | 13.4 | 52.9 | 1.7 | 32.7 | 67.6 | 1.9 | 5.1 |
| S.Meadowell | 0.0 | 13.5 | 8.3 | 96.8 | 85.7 | 10.7 | 8.8 |

Source: North Tyneside Housing Department

The view that problem estates may also be related to design characteristics is one that has gained in popularity in recent years although many of the basic ideas have been in print for some time and can largely be traced to the work of Jane Jacobs in the USA (1961). Her arguments were extended and tested empirically by Oscar Newman (1972) in New York later in the 1960s. Newman was able to demonstrate that various aspects of urban design and layout were associated with criminal acts. More recently Alice Coleman has related anti-social behaviour to modern residential design, drawing particular attention to the problems of 'high-rise' developments (Coleman, 1985). Inevitably, it is those with less power who tend to be allocated the less popular or more problematic housing in terms of design, maintenance and repair (Taylor, 1979).

The third group of theories relate to the nature of communities themselves. Perhaps the main argument here is that there is something in the nature of the community which leads to the development of a kind of sub-culture. Rather than accepting the norms of 'mainstream' society, the community develops its own standards of behaviour. In this way cultural transmission of delinquent behaviour takes place from one generation to the next (Downes, 1966; Mays, 1963; Herbert, 1976). A sub-category of such theories is concerned with the relationship between high population turnover and delinquent behaviour on council estates. Such ideas are closely related to the ecological tradition of the 'Chicago school' of urban sociologists in the 1920s and 1930s where social disorganization was argued to be a product of high mobility, new migrants to the city, high population turnover and the development of a sense of 'anomie' or normlessness. The latter referring to the collapse, in the 'new' urban setting, of the old, traditional norms of control and behaviour (Wirth, 1938). Such conditions were, of course particularly characteristic of the inner city and 'zone of transition'. It is difficult, in areas with a high population turn-over, for a true community to develop as residents may not possess any attachment to place and people. In the absence of such psychological ties, anti-social behaviour to both property and other people may flourish and lead to the development of a problem area.

Previous research (Byrne, 1980) has made much of the design inferiority of Meadowell especially when compared to estates in North Tyneside built under earlier legislation. This perhaps is an unfair comparison, given the major difference in subsidy levels available from central government. More specifically, it would be difficult to argue that the design theory of the origin of problem estates is applicable to Meadowell, at least in the way implied by Coleman. The original Meadowell estate consisted of conventional two-storey dwellings, built in short terraces, and laid out on 'Garden-City' lines, with crescents and cul-de-sacs. There were no multi-storey dwellings on the original Meadowell development. Clearly in these terms, Meadowell does not conform to Coleman's thesis of a design-induced problem estate - Meadowell was not a 'slum on the drawing board' (Benwell Community Project, 1978). However, in true Tyneside tradition, flats constituted the majority of the original dwellings, and there is little doubt that issues such as repair and maintenance have created problems for both the council and tenants (North Tyneside CDP, 1976). But, there is a major difference between inherent design faults and poor management of repairs to existing council stock. The existence of flats and poor maintenance did not cause the Meadowell to become a problem estate, and equally a good repairs service will not solve all of the estate's problems.

The conventionally accepted view of the origins of Meadowell as a problem estate stresses the role of council allocation policies, and the 'dumping' of problematic households in the area (North Tyneside CDP, 1976). In support of this view, reference is usually made to the origins of the estate's original residents. There is clear evidence that council allocation policies have indeed created many problems, especially in the recent past. However, the available data suggests that the initial allocation policy was unlikely to have been the root cause of Meadowell's problems. Yet, as we have stressed, the area is often assumed to have been a problem estate from the very beginning.

There is little doubt, as far as the population of Tyneside at large is concerned, that a mythology has developed surrounding estates such as Meadowell. Quotes, such as the following, are indicative of the perception of such areas as representing a distinctive sub-culture:

> 'Policemen talk of local residents as "scum". They themselves believe that "we are rubbish". This is a sink estate.'

Community worker in North Tyneside quoted in Faith in the City (1985)

The background to such a statement is an assumption by mainstream society that all residents of the area are tainted by some form of anti-social view of life. Yet, such perceptions have wider implications, they permeate life-chances for residents. The same source goes on to observe:

> 'Young people know that there is no point applying for jobs if you live there unless you give a false address.'

(ibid)

In this way, residents of the South Meadowell are distanced from the surrounding area, which therefore influences how they relate to 'outsiders' and how 'outsiders' relate to them. Although such views may be based initially on insubstantial evidence and represent nothing more than local mythology, once ingrained in the local consciousness, such labelling becomes almost impossible to shake-off.

Although all three of these theories have varying degrees of applicability to the case of South Meadowell, one common theme is the way the local population is placed either in a totally passive position (innocent victims of design or dumping), or at best in a reactive position (anti-social sub-culture as a reaction to adverse circumstances). More importantly, such reactions are cast in negative terms. All three theories imply that local people are incapable of acting on their own account in a positive way - helping themselves. Furthermore the label 'problem estate' begs the question 'a problem for whom?' - society, the Council, or the residents? Indeed, to give the Meadowell the all-embracing label of 'problem estate' is to miss the point - to quote a leading resident "We are not a problem estate - we are an estate with problems.". This single observation goes to the core of the problematic; when, and in whose terms can Meadowell be described as a problem estate?

**Meadowell: The Received Wisdom On The Creation Of A Problem Estate.**

A considerable literature on the building and early history of Meadowell estate is in existence (North Tyneside CDP, 1976; 1978; Byrne 1980). A recurrent theme is the unfavourable comparisons that may be drawn between Meadowell and other estates in North Tyneside or the old Tynemouth Borough right from the very origin of the estate. For example, attention has been drawn to the reduced costs in building the first stage of the Meadowell estate (Byrne 1980) and unfavourable comparisons are made with the Balkwell estate, built mainly under the 1919 Housing Act. Meadowell houses certainly were built more cheaply, reflecting to some extent the different levels of central government subsidy available under the Housing Acts. A comparison of any estates built under the 1919 and 1930 Housing Acts is bound to reflect badly on the latter, but it is all too easy to imply that lower spending automatically led to the creation of a 'problem estate'. Indeed. it is clear that the average cost of the Meadowell dwellings of £350 was well in line with the national average (Bowley, 1945).

However, other processes were at work in Tynemouth which, it has been frequently cited, led to the development of Meadowell as a problem estate from the very start. Two factors appear to be important. First was the fact that Meadowell was an estate initially built by the local authority for allocation to slum clearance tenants. A specific issue associated with this role was the policy of insisting upon the disinfestation of new tenants and their belongings. Second, in addition to the initial slum-clearance role, the estate rapidly acquired another function - that of the relief of overcrowding throughout the Borough, whether in slum clearance areas or not.

As already noted, the origin of the Meadowell estate lies with the 1930 (Greenwood) Housing Act, aimed primarily at the provision of council housing for slum clearance tenants rather than for general needs. The way that the Tynemouth Borough Council responded to this central government initiative is extremely significant. In fact, the council re-formed its Housing Committee in 1930, having abandoned it in 1928 (Price, 1988)! Quite clearly, at this stage, the council's commitment to local authority housing was at least open to question. Up until the early 1930s the private sector, despite its historical failure, was still seen as the means by which housing provision should take place, as an editorial in the Shields Daily News proclaimed: "...it is desirable that the building of subsidised houses should cease..." (Shields Daily News, 26 March, 1932). However, the council responded enthusiastically to the 1930 Act, deciding to build 850 dwellings in 5 years under the Act and a further 200 'general needs' houses under the 1924 (Wheatley) Act. Largely as a result of this activity 9454 individuals were cleared from slum properties between 1932 and 1938 (MOH Reports, Tynemouth CB). Although Meadowell did not absorb this total number, it was the only estate specifically built to house slum-clearance tenants. Building of Meadowell commenced in 1933, and allocation policy was as follows:

> "The Transfer of Tenants from Slum Clearance Areas" -
>
> The report of the Medical officer of Health on the general question of the transfer of tenants from the slum clearance areas to the houses now being erected on the Ridges Estate was received. The Medical Officer recommended (a) that every tenant in the slum clearance areas with children should be automatically offered one of the new houses on the Ridges Estate"

(Tynemouth Co. Borough, Minutes of Housing Committee, April 19th, 1933).

As part of its allocation procedures, Tynemouth Borough introduced a controversial policy with regard to the Meadowell Estate; that of enforced disinfestation of new Meadowell tenants who originated from slum clearance areas. This had significant implications for the way the estate was perceived by the public at large, both in the 1930s and subsequently:

> "There is considerable speculation....as to how Tynemouth Corporation is going to deal with the knotty problems surrounding the transference of families from the slum clearance areas of North Shields.... In particular, the problem of preventing the perhaps unwilling introduction of vermin to the new property has exercised the minds of the authorities, who realise the matter is a delicate one."

(Shields Daily News, May 26th, 1933)

As the same policy of disinfestation did not apply to 'general needs' tenants, an immediate dichotomy developed within Tynemouth estates, and the process of 'labelling' of residents of Meadowell began. Not unnaturally they were perceived as 'dirty' by many of their fellow citizens, regardless of their actual state of cleanliness and hygiene.

A second factor in the development of the estate's reputation and character was that the local authority rehoused people from overcrowded housing elsewhere in Tynemouth into Meadowell:

> "The Transfer of Tenants from Slum Clearance Areas" -
>
> (b) that where accommodation is required for tenants in the slum clearance areas consisting of one or two persons, such cases should receive special consideration by this Committee, in order that the best use should be made, from the general health point of view, of the new accommodation available. In dealing with this class of tenant, the Medical Officer suggested that the landlords of tenements in the Borough where there is at present overcrowding, which cannot be abated owing to lack of alternative accommodation might be approached to see if the families from such overcrowded privately owned tenements could be transferred to the new Corporation houses, and tenants from the slum clearance areas consisting of two persons or less transferred to the privately owned tenements, to the mutual benefit of all concerned."

(Tynemouth Co. Borough, Minutes of Housing Committee, April 19th, 1933)

Allocation policy therefore included both residents of slum areas alone and overcrowded households elsewhere, especially those with children. Inevitably, therefore, a concentration of large families took place on Meadowell. This played a significant part in the development of overcrowding in some of Meadowell's dwellings, and the reputation of the area in housing unusually large families became an important ingredient in the labelling of the estate - large families (in the popular public imagination of the 1920s and 1930s) being increasingly associated with the lower social orders and tendencies towards fecklessness and overpopulation.

Another factor in the local perception of Meadowell's unsavoury reputation related to the origins of the tenants and particularly that, as much of the slum property cleared in the 1930s was on the banks of the river Tyne, (Cameron and Crompton, op.cit.), many of the new slum clearance tenants on Meadowell belonged to the sea-faring or fishing community. As much of this 'community' was characterised by households lacking visible male heads for parts of the year but having large numbers of children, unfavourable judgements were easy to make about the morality of lone females left at home whilst their 'men' went to sea.

These processes and perceptions created a reputation for Meadowell as a high density, slum clearance estate containing tenants of dubious morality. In short, an area which in many respects, was outside the norms of mainstream society. Many of the accounts of the development of Meadowell assume that this reputation was an accurate reflection of reality and that the area was a 'problem estate' from its inception. Yet this view is questionable on a number of counts. We will argue that the root causes of Meadowell's present problems cannot be attributed to the specific processes that were operative at the time of the estate's establishment and are much more recent phenomena. Meadowell certainly did house relatively poor and deprived people from the very beginning but that does not mean that it was a problem estate from the very beginning. Indeed, as the following section argues, it is possible to form an entirely different, much more favourable and optimistic view of Meadowell in the 1930s.

Meadowell: An alternative view of its early years.

One illustration of local opinion about Meadowell in its early years can be found in a piece of 'investigative journalism' on the newly built estate. This was full of praise, both for the dwellings and the cleanliness of the inhabitants:

> '....I had a thorough walk around the Ridges estate, the sun was shining,....and the atmosphere was full of optimism. The first resident I decided to have a few words with....invited me inside the living room to have a look at the house. The room....was neatness itself with new furniture in the best of taste'

(Shields Daily News, 12th May 1934).

For many of the new residents, movement into the estate represented a substantial increase in accommodation standards. Therefore it is difficult to understand how, even if the Meadowell was built to lower standards than previous estates in the area, by moving people into better accommodation, this could create a problem estate. The 'problem' in terms of housing infrastructure already existed in much worse form in the slums of Tynemouth. In the eyes of many of the arriving tenants the houses represented a new and welcome opportunity to improve their life-chances in a much cleaner and healthier environment.

A second perspective on the new estate may be gained from the views of Tynemouth's Medical Officer of Health. Some writers argue that slums are the product of their inhabitants, although in the case of Meadowell, the borough's medical officer emphatically disputed this point. As the key figure in the implementation of the slum clearance policy he was the one official most likely to have had considerable familiarity with the tenants and their conditions. He was well satisfied with the standards of the early occupants of Meadowell:

> 'The cleanliness and tidiness of the dwelling houses on the new estate more than confirms my opinions that slums are not the product of the inhabitants."

(MOH Annual Report, 1934).

One of Tynemouth Borough's chief professional officers was therefore convinced that the residents moving from Tynemouth's slums were not intrinsically 'problem tenants', and were taking good care of their new dwellings. In addition, data on rent arrears soon after the completion of the estate does not suggest any particular problems. In the year 1934/5 the average level of collection from the whole of the Tynemouth Borough's council estates was 99.7%, for the 96 self-contained houses on Meadowell it was 99.3% and for the slum clearance properties (largely flats) it was 98.4%. The council pronounced itself satisfied with this level of arrears (County Borough of Tynemouth, Proceedings of the Council, 1934/5).

From such evidence it would appear then that the quality of slum clearance tenants did not lead to a detrimental effect on the estate as has been previously supposed. Equally importantly, the quantity of new tenants originating from slum-housing on the steep banks overlooking the river has been exaggerated. Meadowell is usually assumed to have been exclusively populated from the latter districts which have also been characterised by quite specific socio-economic characteristics:

> "...an explicit contrast was often made between the banksides and the areas at the tops of the banks, which were described as 'decent mean streets'. The contrast was not just in terms of housing conditions but in terms of the occupational and income characteristics of the respective populations. The bank-toppers were typically skilled shipyard craftsmen and the Medical Officer of Health in his evidence made it clear that it was from these more affluent workers, rather than from slum dwellers, that the residents of the Balkwell estate had been drawn."

(North Tyneside CDP, 1976)

The implication is clear - Balkwell residents originated from the bank tops and were largely skilled manual workers, whereas Meadowell residents originated from the bank sides and were in mainly semi and unskilled manual occupations.

It was not the case that Meadowell was wholly populated by former residents of the 'bank side'. In fact, of the 3641 persons affected by slum clearance only 31% came from the immediate riverside area (54th Annual Report, Medical Officer of Health, Tynemouth County Borough, 1934). Although the vast majority of those affected by slum clearance would be rehoused in Meadowell as this was virtually the only 'slum clearance' estate in Tynemouth at this time, less than one third could possibly have come from the river banks. It appears that the origins of Meadowell's first residents were considerably more diverse than has often been supposed. The Medical Officer of Health had pointed to the same conclusion in 1931 when he noted that "...in North Shields, Preston, Tynemouth and Cullercoats there were many houses which were quite unfit for human habitation." (Shields Daily News, 7 July, 1931).

In addition, the usual interpretation of the likely employment characteristics of Meadowell's early residents is called into question by the existence of this wider catchment. The local press noted in 1934, for example, that "...some people now living on the estate once had shops which were wiped out by the slum clearance..." (Shields Daily News, 26 April, 1934). In particular, the proposition that the newly built estate housed a large number of sea-farers is difficult to sustain. Other data sources point to a similar conclusion. The compilation of the Electoral Register for 1946 was of course complicated by the absence in the forces or at sea of many eligible voters. These individuals were recorded in a separate Service Register. Registration may not have been comprehensive but on the whole of the Meadowell estate only seven seamen were recorded. This is not to deny that the employment structure of Meadowell was likely to be dominated by unskilled and semi-skilled manual employment. In the absence of a comprehensive data source we simply do not know, but the assertion that jobs associated with the sea-faring trades formed a major segment of the employment structure appears not to be the case.

One final piece of evidence on the reality of Meadowell at this early stage may be examined. In the literature on so-called problem estates the issue of high population turnover and the subsequent lack of community development is frequently cited as characteristic. In fact, the objective evidence suggests that Meadowell was no more problematic in this sense than most other areas. Table 2 indicates the level of mobility from 1939 to 1949 as indicated by the Electoral Registers, a period when high mobility may have been expected due to the war years. 'No change' means that exactly the same adults were living at the same address at the later date as in the earlier year. 'Partial turnover' means that at least one adult name was in common at both dates, and 'Total change' indicates that all the

**TABLE 2**

**TURNOVER RATES IN SOUTH MEADOWELL, 1939-1949**

| Date | No Change | | Partial Turnover | | Total Change | |
|---|---|---|---|---|---|---|
| | No. | % | No. | % | No. | % |
| 1939-46 | 251 | 38.0 | 281 | 42.6 | 128 | 19.4 |
| 1946-49 | 261 | 34.1 | 350 | 45.7 | 155 | 20.2 |

Source: Electoral Registers

previous names had gone. A turnover rate of about 20% in the seven years between 1939 and 1946 does not seem inordinately high and, in fact, compares favourably with studies elsewhere. In Leicester, for example, in the equivalent period annual turnover rates were between 5% and 10% (Pritchard, 1976). Furthermore, there is no lack of evidence of community spirit and organisations on

Meadowell at this time. For example, a request from local residents to establish a Boy Scout meeting hut was made to the Council in 1937 (Council Proceedings, 24 March, 1937) and, certainly by the end of the war a Tenants' Association existed (Council Proceedings, 1951).

Our analysis so far has revealed that in the 1930s the Meadowell acquired a poor local reputation. Once that reputation was established, it became almost impossible to prevent its perpetuation. In other words, the Meadowell estate became a victim of labelling (Damer, 1974; Gill, 1977). However, the analysis has also demonstrated that this reputation was in many respects undeserved, and not based on the objective reality of Meadowell in the 1930s. The fundamental question that remains to be answered, therefore, is why did this labelling occur and why did it prove, ultimately, to be a more powerful influence on the fate of the estate than objective reality ?

**Meadowell in a Wider Context: Housing and Society in Tynemouth.**

The debate at a local level on the character of slum dwellers and the appropriate nature of replacement accommodation for such people was certain to be influenced and perhaps even shaped by the national perspective on such issues. This national perspective was very powerfully shaped by the pervasive moral tone surrounding most urban issues from the mid Victorian period onwards. It has been argued, for example, (Davidoff and Hall, 1987) that the nature of middle class suburbia was itself formed by those Victorian values which were in turn a response to the many evils produced by the early nineteenth century urbanisation process. Thus, the emphasis on sobriety, domestic privacy, religious observance, thrift and cleanliness endowed the domestic sphere with a moral purpose. This was best achieved within the confines of a disciplined nuclear family where privacy ensured a lack of contamination from dangerous external influences. From the viewpoint of this private world of the middle class suburbs the slums, with their conspicuous lack of domestic privacy, were the very antithesis of satisfactory domestic arrangements. It followed that the people living in them must therefore lack many of the moral qualities Victorian society deemed to be so necessary. Because of their domestic arrangements, to many middle class observers, slum dwellers could not be anything other than unregenerate. In this way a clear link was made between the physical and environmental conditions prevalent in certain areas and the social and moral ills of society. The slum came to be defined not only in environmental terms but also with reference to the moral character of its inhabitants (Gaskell, 1990).

The particular characteristics of the slums and especially the slum dwellers were thrown into sharper relief by the distinctions made within the working class. This is sometimes rather simply represented as the distinction between the 'deserving' and 'undeserving' poor. Even amongst the so-called 'labour aristocracy' there existed a distinct hierarchy of skilled trades (Crossick, 1978). Such status distinctions were reinforced on Tyneside because of the method of organising work in some of the principal industries, most notably ship-building. Traditionally, each skilled worker would have his 'gang' of semi-skilled workers, labourers, and apprentices, working directly under his supervision. This stratification at work inevitably had some impact upon the residential sphere and seems likely to have led to a similar stratification of housing areas. Certainly, those who could afford it would surely seek to escape or distance themselves from the housing areas identified as the 'worst' neighbourhoods. Yet, for many, if the local housing supply remained highly constrained, the means of such 'escape' would obviously be strictly limited, frustrating the objectives of those who sought respectability in a new location. The poorest slum dwellers were therefore often doubly condemned, first because it was believed that their life-styles did not conform to the widely accepted norms of respectability and morality, and secondly, in periods or geographical areas of housing shortage, because they were held to 'contaminate' adjacent areas and social groups (see Gaskell, op. cit., p. 24). Perceived resentment against slum dwellers was therefore likely to have been greater amongst those who came into contact with them more, rather than amongst the more distant middle classes. Thus, different groups saw the slums and slum dwellers in a negative light but for rather different reasons. In Tynemouth, both factors were to play a part in the characterisation of the residents of an estate such as Meadowell, built primarily for former slum dwellers.

It is clear, therefore, that we must examine processes operating within the wider Tynemouth housing market in order to understand the early and persistently negative perception of the Meadowell estate. The argument developed here is that Meadowell residents were, as we have already seen, very easy to label as being 'different' and 'problematic' and characteristic of the 'undeserving poor' yet, in the very difficult housing market circumstances of Tynemouth in the 1930s, they appeared to be obtaining some sort of preferential treatment. It appeared that housing was being built for 'them' on a scale not previously seen at a time when many other types of households (usually perceived as 'decent' households) were struggling in the housing market. The reasons for this are complex but relate to the combination of an historically dreadful legacy of inadequate housing, an extremely sluggish response from the local supply side especially when related to need, and the specifically beneficial circumstances under which housing for slum clearance and overcrowded households could be developed by the local authority under the 1930 Housing Act. Added to this combination was the deep-rooted concern over the moral condition of such people when compared to the more 'respectable' elements in society. In other words, factors entirely external to Meadowell combined to create an environment within which a negative perception of that area developed. To understand the way this perception came about it is necessary to establish the nature of the Tynemouth housing market in the late nineteenth and early twentieth centuries.

The existence of high levels of housing stress on Tyneside at the turn of the century is well documented (Cameron and Crompton, op. cit. p.120) and Tynemouth County Borough shared most of the problems exhibited elsewhere in the region. Amongst the most significant were high levels of overcrowding. Table 3 shows the dimensions of the problem. The proportion of the population living at a density of more than two persons per room decreases by 1931, albeit to a still high 16.9% but the main feature remains the very high level of overcrowding experienced by many Tynemouth households.

**TABLE 3**

**CROWDING OF POPULATION AND FAMILIES, TYNEMOUTH C.B., 1911-1931**

| | 1911 | 1921 | 1931 |
|---|---|---|---|
| % of population at 2+ per room | 30.7 | 28.4 | 16.9 |
| Population in 1 room only | 4064 | 5814 | 5513 |
| Population in 1 or 2 rooms | 17261 | 21133 | 19321 |
| Families in 1 room only | 1423 | 1917 | 1887 |
| Families in 1 or 2 rooms | 4552 | 5440 | 5429 |

Source: Census Volumes, 1911, 1921, 1931

The causes of overcrowding may vary from area to area. In some cases it may be due to a disproportionately large number of large families. In such cases, even though the size of dwellings may be similar to or above the national average, overcrowding may result. In other cases overcrowding may be explained by a disproportionate share of small houses, resulting in quite small families experiencing overcrowded living conditions. Table 4 provides some basic data on family size and dwelling size.

**TABLE 4**

**FAMILY SIZE AND DWELLING SIZE, TYNEMOUTH C.B., 1911-1931**

| | 1911 | | 1921 | | 1931 | |
|---|---|---|---|---|---|---|
| Family size | no. | % | no. | % | no. | % |
| 1 | 724 | 5.7 | 773 | 5.6 | 1093 | 6.8 |
| 2 | 1876 | 14.8 | 2113 | 15.3 | 3145 | 19.1 |
| 3-4 | 4585 | 36.4 | 5128 | 37.3 | 6752 | 42.0 |
| 5-7 | 4234 | 33.5 | 4405 | 32.0 | 4340 | 27.0 |
| 7+ | 1217 | 9.6 | 1355 | 9.8 | 749 | 4.6 |
| Dwelling size(rooms) | | | | | | |
| 1 | 1423 | 11.3 | 1917 | 13.9 | 1887 | 11.7 |
| 2 | 3129 | 24.8 | 3523 | 25.6 | 3542 | 22.0 |
| 3-4 | 5104 | 40.4 | 5461 | 39.6 | 6508 | 40.5 |
| 5+ | 2980 | 23.6 | 2873 | 20.9 | 4142 | 25.8 |

Source: Census Volumes, 1911, 1921, 1931

Over the two decades the number of larger families declines as one would expect for this period. Although Tynemouth had some very large families at all three dates Table 4 does not suggest that, on average, family size was inordinately large. Indeed, at all three dates the majority of families were of four people or less. In contrast, it is clear that Tynemouth was characterised by small dwelling size. Houses of one and two rooms formed a significant proportion of the dwelling stock. Hardly surprisingly, the proportion of Tynemouth's population and families living in these extremely small dwellings remained high at all three dates. Never less than one third of families were in dwellings of one or two rooms only. It seems, therefore, that small dwelling size was a far more important factor in explaining Tynemouth's overcrowding than family size. This is confirmed in Table 5 which compares the structure of dwelling size in Tynemouth with England and Wales for 1931. Whilst the proportion of very large houses of nine rooms or more is very similar, the proportion of dwellings of three or less rooms in Tynemouth is more than double the national proportion.

**TABLE 5**

**DWELLING SIZE IN TYNEMOUTH AND ENGLAND AND WALES, 1931**

| Dwelling size | % of dwellings | |
|---|---|---|
| | Tynemouth | England and Wales |
| 1-3 rooms | 38.3 | 15.2 |
| 4-5 rooms | 42.1 | 52.9 |
| 6-8 rooms | 15.3 | 27.4 |
| 9+ rooms | 4.3 | 4.5 |

Source: Census Volumes, 1931

The Tynemouth housing market in the years leading up to and immediately on the eve of the building of Meadowell was therefore characterised by very high levels of overcrowding and a high proportion of very small dwellings. The range of households experiencing poor housing conditions was therefore likely to have been considerable, a factor which formed a very important component of the 'external environment' within which Meadowell emerged and helped to shape attitudes towards the estate and its residents.

Inevitably, in specific localities within the Tynemouth area conditions were especially bad:

> 'The effect of bad arrangements of the houses or the narrowness or bad arrangement of the streets is to exclude sun and light and air, to produce dampness, bad ventilation and faulty drainage, and to prevent free circulation of air. Access to houses is rendered difficult and there is serious congestion of houses and persons. The facilities and means for obtaining a healthy standard of living are not available for the inhabitants of the area.'

(Medical Officer of Health, Clive Street Public Inquiry, 1933)

Thus, in the Clive Street clearance area in 1933 the death rate was 20.8 per 1000 population, compared to a rate of 12.8 for the County Borough as a whole. The infant mortality rate was 143 per 1000 whilst the average for the whole local authority was 83 (North Tyneside CDP, 1978). The nature of another clearance area, the Liddle Street area, was described as follows:

> 'one thoroughfare, Union Stairs, housed 48 inhabitants living in 17 rooms with one water tap for all of them. In Liddle Street itself there were 405 inhabitants. Only two of the dwellings had separate internal water supplies. There was one tap for every 23 people and one privy (earth) for every 11 people. There were no baths..'

(North Tyneside CDP, 1978)

Between 1932 and 1936 Tynemouth Council served 33 Compulsory Purchase Orders in such areas in order to carry out slum clearance. Some 9454 people were living in such areas. The vast majority were, of course, likely to have been overcrowded but the living conditions for those who were not seem likely to have been almost as bad. In each year between 1920 and 1933 never less than one-fifth of Tynemouth's babies were born in single-roomed houses (Goodfellow, 1940), peaking at well over one-third in the mid 1920s. It was not just at the time of inquiries into specific slum clearance areas that concern was expressed at the state of much of the accommodation available. For example, the Medical Officer of Health's annual reports frequently drew attention to the problems:

> 'Structural defects are prominent in most of the tenement dwellings, and the overcrowding which is present in some houses is bound to produce a moral as well as a physical degeneration among the overcrowded inhabitants.'

(Medical Officer of Health, Annual Report, 1930, p.86)

The evidence available appears to suggest that a significant proportion of Tynemouth's working class experienced appalling housing conditions. This phenomenon does not seem to have been isolated to the unskilled or semi-skilled groups alone but is likely to have been more widespread than that. For example, only 12.8% of the occupations in Tynemouth 1931 were listed as 'general labourer' but 38% of the dwellings were of three rooms or less, that is, very small houses. Over 35% of occupations were 'white collar' or middle class occupations whilst larger houses of six rooms or more constituted 19.6% of the housing stock. On this basis, skilled manual workers and artisans seem likely to have overlapped with their less skilled counterparts and to have been competing with them for very small houses. It is this factor which explains the very high degree of subdivision of available housing stock. The Medical Officer of Health reported in 1932:

> 'The disconcerting feature. is the large increase in the number of families living three or more to a dwelling. Whatever the cause, there is a very large increase in the numbers of houses occupied by multiple tenancies.'

(Tynemouth C.B., MOH Annual Report, 1932, p.xiii)

Having established the highly problematic nature of the structure of Tynemouth's housing market at the time when the Meadowell estate was built, it remains to discuss some of the dynamics of change, especially the relationship between supply and demand. Table 6 shows the change in the number of families recorded in the census in Tynemouth C.B. from 1901 to 1931 and the number of houses built. Taking these figures at face value it would appear that there was a shortfall of 360 dwellings in the 1901-1911 period, 330 in the 1911-1921 period and only 14 in the 1921-1931 period. However, this is to ignore the already poor state of accommodation available at the turn of the century and the necessity for replacement dwellings to make good such shortcomings. Furthermore, it is to assume that the census definition of 'families' is an accurate one. In fact it is extremely likely that a high proportion of 'hidden' families existed, that is, families sharing, lodging with other families, or living with relatives but recorded along with their co-residents as one family. The real level of household demand is likely to have been much higher than that indicated by the increase in 'families' recorded in the census at this time. For example, the marriage rate is a clear indication of new household formation and therefore latent demand within the housing market. Between 1901 and 1911 there were over 5,000 marriages within Tynemouth County Borough (calculated from the Registrar General's Annual Returns) and between 1921 and 1931 over 4,000. For those newly formed households who remained in the borough, sharing with other families and in-laws must have provided the main source of accommodation. The vice-chairman of the Housing Committee reported in June 1931 that there were over 1,000 families on the waiting list for the 104 houses then being built on the Balkwell estate (Shields Daily News, 22 June, 1931). Given the local housing situation however, many locally born people chose to migrate elsewhere. Between 1921 and 1931, natural increase within the borough would have led to a population growth of 5,804. The actual growth was only 1,152, implying a net out-migration of 4,652 people.

**TABLE 6**

**CHANGE IN NUMBER OF FAMILIES AND HOUSEBUILDING, TYNEMOUTH C.B. 1911-1931**

| Change in number of families | | Numbers of houses built |
|---|---|---|
| 1901 - 1911 | + 1783 | 1423 |
| 1911 - 1921 | + 991 | 259+ (*) |
| 1921 - 1931 | + 2305 | 2291 |

(*) plus a few houses built during the war years

Source: Annual Reports, MOH, Tynemouth C.B.

It is quite clear therefore, that the supply-side response to the demand for accommodation was especially sluggish in the Tynemouth area and this helps to explain the appalling housing situation that had developed at the end of the nineteenth century and the beginning of the twentieth. However, the analysis so far has omitted two further important factors, these being the loss of accommodation over these years due to demolition or conversion to other uses and the existence of vacant dwellings. It appears that the former process was quite significant and that the number of vacancies was surprisingly high (about 200) given the high level of demand for accommodation. Both factors mean that the relationship of the number of houses built (Table 6) to real need was even more adverse. Table 7, drawn from the 1931 census, demonstrates some of these features and provides a picture of a housing market situation under extreme stress. Despite the house building that had taken place, the increase in occupied dwellings between 1921 and 1931 was only 420, due to vacancy and the loss of housing by demolition and conversion. At the same time, the excess of families over dwellings occupied increased by 1,885. For the 83 County Boroughs listed in England and Wales this represented the third 'worst' performance in terms of the increase in occupied dwellings.

**TABLE 7**

**1931 CENSUS INDICATORS OF TYNEMOUTH C.B. HOUSING SITUATION**

| | | |
|---|---|---|
| Excess of private families over dwellings occupied, | 1921 | 856 |
| Excess of private families over dwellings occupied, | 1931 | 2741 |
| Private families per occupied dwelling, | 1921 | 1.07 |
| Private families per occupied dwelling, | 1931 | 1.21 |
| Increase in number of occupied dwellings, | 1921 - 1931 | 420 |

Source: 1931 Census Volumes

The conclusion is therefore inescapable. In the face of a continuing and self-evident housing problem, the dimensions of which were clearly apparent from official statistics and the Medical Officer's Reports, the response of the local housebuilding industry in both the private and public sectors was woefully inadequate up to the early 1930s. Indeed, had outward migration not relieved some of the pressure on the local housing market, the situation would have reached crisis proportions. It is against this background that the 1930 Housing Act was implemented in Tynemouth, the Act which led to the building of Meadowell.

## Conclusion: manufacturing the myth.

The implementation of the 1930 Act was preceded by a considerable debate on the financial issues involved, a debate which revealed the distinction which was clearly being made in the minds of many between the kind of housing which was appropriate for former slum dwellers and that appropriate for the rest of the population. This distinction, which has frequently been pointed out at the national scale (for example, Ravetz, 1974; National CDP, 1976) was given an extra dimension in Tynemouth C.B. because of the generally parlous state of the local housing market, not just for slum dwellers, but also for many others. The fact that the Housing Committee chose to build conventional two storey dwellings (albeit in flats) rather than several storey blocks of flats caused a furore amongst the cost-conscious council members who claimed that "...Corporation policy is inflicting an unfair burden on the thrifty members of the community. It is rotten business, rotten finance, and in every way fundamentally unsound..." (Shields Daily News, 25 June, 1931). A similar theme was apparent early in 1932 when a Shields Daily News editorial under the headline 'We Want a Reduction in Rates' precipitated a spate of letters, mainly complaining at the levels of public spending (Shields Daily News, 22 March, 1932; 29 March, 1932; 6 April, 1932). Although falling short of outright opposition, the local press left its readers in no doubt over its attitude to the proposals for building the new replacement housing for slum dwellers:

> 'It is not an equitable state of affairs that one section of the community should be housed partly at the expense of the State and the municipality, while others have to pay the full market value of their house accommodation...'

(Shields Daily News, 26 March, 1932)

Thus, even before the Meadowell estate was built and the first residents moved in, a climate of opinion was developing which placed such residents in a negative light. They were clearly benefiting from public expenditure, for many households not so benefiting the local housing situation was extremely problematic, yet 'they' could be characterised as the least deserving of recipients. Resentment therefore formed a significant part of the labelling of Meadowell from the very beginning.

Once the estate was built, given the circumstances by which it was peopled and the local authority's policy in relation to issues such as disinfestation, this labelling appeared to become self-justifying and the mythology of Meadowell was born. Within a year of the building of the estate a leading article in the local newspaper proclaimed 'We Must Fight the Slum State of Mind' in relation to the re-housing of slum dwellers and revealed openly many of the concerns discussed above:

> '...without some sort of very definite education and guidance, you cannot expect them to live above the slum level - a level that is a grave physical and moral danger to the community.'

(Shields Daily News, 1 May, 1934)

Although not explicitly stated, the article can only have been a reference to Meadowell and it is noteworthy for two reasons. First, that 'physical' danger is now being added to the previously recognised 'moral' danger emanating from areas where the 'slum mentality' is held to prevail and, second, that within less than a year of the building of Meadowell, the fears formerly expressed about the overcrowded riverside slum districts have now been transferred to the new estate. Yet this is despite the considerable evidence of a more optimistic nature that exists on the early character of Meadowell, evidence we have already drawn attention to.

It seems that the estate and its residents could not win. Regardless of the objective reality, a significant and influential body of opinion had already determined that the area was a 'problem' and was bound to be a problem because of the nature of the people who moved there and the nature of the areas they moved from. Arguably, much of the subsequent history of the estate has seen a gradual convergence of label and reality (Barke and Turnbull, 1992) yet, given a more sympathetic external environment in which to develop, there would have been nothing particularly inevitable about this convergence. Of course, Meadowell would never have been a particular 'blue riband' estate but the myth that Meadowell was a problem from the beginning was born partially out of the Victorian influences which conceived of former slum dwellers in a particular way, partially out of the specific local circumstances in dealing with the first tenants, and partially out of resentment which itself stemmed from the desperate local housing situation for many in the borough. It was the latter factor which added a particular edge to the perception of Meadowell elsewhere in the Tynemouth area. Although it is difficult to claim that it was an overt or conscious determination, it can be argued that it became psychologically necessary for the middle classes and skilled working classes to 'manufacture' Meadowell as a problem and, of course, it was an easy target. By so characterising the estate a distinctive 'sense of place' was created (for those outside; there was of course a very different sense of place for those inside) and the geographical association between a certain place and a certain type of people became fixed. The boundary of Meadowell became a precise definition of 'inside' and 'outside', between 'us' and 'them'. Furthermore, this neat way of fitting a label to a particular place and a particular group of people became almost an explanation in itself. To many ordinary citizens of Tynemouth C.B. the residents of Meadowell possessed specific characteristics, if they did not possess those characteristics then they would not live on Meadowell. Such attribution and the labelling that it implied was a satisfactory way of psychologically containing the problem as well as, subsequently (through the allocation mechanism), of physically containing it. The message to be read on the label was clear - this place, and these people, are different; they and it are 'a problem'.

**Michael Barke**

**Guy Turnbull**

**Plate 15.**
Early photograph of the Meadowell Estate, North Shields.

**Plates 16 and 17.**
Recent photographs of the same area.

## References


Archbishop of Canterbury's Commission on Urban Priority Areas, (1985), Faith in the City, Church House Publishing, London.

Baldwin, J. (1975), Urban criminality and the problem estate, Local Government Studies, vol. 1, pp.12-20.

Barke, M. and Turnbull, G. (1992) Meadowell: The Biography of an 'Estate with Problems', Gower, London

Benwell Community Project, (1978), Slums on the Drawing Board, Final Report Series, No. 4, Benwell Community Project, Newcastle upon Tyne.

Bowley, M. (1945) Housing and the State, George Allen and Unwin, London

Byrne, D. (1980), The standard of council housing in inter-war North Shields - a case study in the politics of reproduction, in Melling, J. (ed.) Housing, Social Policy and the State, Croom Helm, London, pp.168-93.

Cameron, S. and Crompton, P. (1988), Housing, in, Robinson, F. (ed) Post - Industrial Tyneside, Newcastle upon Tyne City Libraries, Newcastle upon Tyne.

Campbell, B. (1991), Kings of the Road, Marxism Today, December, pp.20-23

Coleman, A. (1985), Utopia on Trial, Hilary Shipman, London.

Crossick, G. (1978) An Artisan Elite in Victorian Society, Croom Helm, London

Damer, S. (1974) Wine Alley: the sociology of a dreadful enclosure, Sociological Review, vol. 22, pp.221-48

Davidoff, L. and Hall, C. (1987) Family Fortunes: Men and Women of the English Middle Class, 1780 - 1850, Hutchinson, London

Downes, D.M. (1966), The Delinquent Solution, Routledge and Kegan Paul, London.

English, J. (1979), Access and deprivation in local authority housing, in Jones, C. (ed) Urban Deprivation and the Inner City, Croom Helm, London

Gaskell, M. (ed) (1990), Slums, Leicester University Press, London

Gill, O. (1977), Luke Street, Macmillan, London.

Goodfellow, D. (1940), Tyneside: The Social Facts, Co-operative Printing Society, Newcastle upon Tyne.

Gray, F. (1976), Selection and allocation in council housing, Transactions, Institute of British Geographers, New Series, vol. 1, no. 1, pp.36-46.

Herbert, D.T. (1976), The study of delinquency areas: a social geographical approach, Transactions, Institute of British Geographers, New Series, vol. 1, no. 4, pp.472-92

Jacobs, J. (1961), The Death and Life of Great American Cities, Vintage Books, New York

Mays, J.B. (1963), Delinquency areas: a re-assessment, British Journal of Criminology, vol.3, pp.216-30.

National Community Development Project, (1976), Whatever Happened to Council Housing? CDP Information and Intelligence Unit, London.

Newman, O. (1972), Defensible Space, Macmillan, London.

North Tyneside CDP, (1976), The Meadowell - the history of a 1930s housing estate, in, Some Housing and Town Planning Issues in North Tyneside, North Tyneside CDP, North Shields, pp.104-24

North Tyneside CDP (1978), North Shields: Working Class Politics and Housing, 1900 - 1977, Final Report, vol. 1, North Tyneside CDP,North Shields.

Price, N. (1988), Housing Access and the Marginal Poor, unpublished M.A. Thesis, Newcastle upon Tyne Polytechnic, Newcastle upon Tyne.

Pritchard, R.M. (1976), Housing and the Spatial Structure of the City, Cambridge University Press, Cambridge

Ravetz, A. (1974) From working class tenement to modern flat: local authorities and multi-storey housing between the wars, in Sutcliffe, A. (ed) Multi-Storey Living: The British Working Class Experience, Croom Helm, London

Taylor, P.J. (1979), 'Difficult-to-let', 'difficult-to-live-in', and sometimes 'difficult-to-get-out-of': an essay on the provision of council housing, with special reference to Killingworth, Environment and Planning A, vol 11, pp.1305-1320

Taylor, P.J. and Hadfield, H. (1982), Housing and the state: a case study and structuralist interpretation, in Cox, K.R and Johnston, R.J. (eds) Conflict, Politics and the Urban Scene, Longman, London, pp.241-63.

Turnbull, G.M. (forthcoming), The Role of Socio-Spatial Processes in the Youth Labour Market: The Case of North Tyneside, unpublished Ph. D. thesis, Newcastle upon Tyne Polytechnic, Newcastle upon Tyne

Wirth, L. (1938), Urbanism as a way of life, American Journal of Sociology, vol. 44, pp.1-24.

## About the Authors

DR MICHAEL BARKE obtained a BA Honours degree in geography from Liverpool University and a Ph.D from Glasgow University for work on the historical geography of Scottish towns. His interest in the historical aspects of housing development on Tyneside arose from work undertaken for the Benwell Community Development Project. He is the joint author of Newcastle's Changing Map and Meadowell: The Biography of "An Estate with Problems". Research interests include the geography of social change in North East England with particular reference to housing.

DAVID BYRNE studied at Newcastle University and the London School of Economics. He is Senior Lecturer in Social Policy at the University of Durham and a Labour councillor in Gateshead. His numerous writings include contributions to CDP reports, a recent study of a Tyneside Inner City area and he is also one of the contributors to Geordies: Roots of Regionalism, R Colls and B Lancaster (eds), Edinburgh, 1992.

MAUREEN CALLCOTT was Senior Lecturer in History at Newcastle Polytechnic (University of Northumbria) teaching Modern British and European History. She now teaches part-time for the Open University. Her research has included the municipal government of Newcastle upon Tyne in the Victorian period, political developments in the north east in the twentieth century and various aspects of women's history. She is currently editing the diaries of Ruth Dodds of Gateshead.

BILL LANCASTER was born in a Tyneside flat and studied at the University of Warwick where he obtained a PhD in 1982. His publications include Radicalism Co-operation and Socialism, Leicester 1987, Life and Labour in a 20th century city, 1986, with Tony Mason and Geordies: Roots of Regionalism, edited with R Colls. He is currently Senior Lecturer in Social History at the University of Northumbria.

KIT PEARCE obtained a BA Honours degree in English and History and an MA in Housing Policy and Management at the University of Northumbria. He is currently employed as a housing officer on Derwentside.

MR GUY TURNBULL is currently writing a PhD thesis on the uneven impact of Youth Training Schemes in North Tyneside. As part of this research, close involvement with Community Groups on the Meadowell estate has developed. He is particularly interested in local economic development and the role of co-operative and community initiatives in this process. He is a graduate in geography from the University of Northumbria at Newcastle.

# Index